Joyful Parent =
Happy Home

by

Mary Hudson

Harrison House
Tulsa, OK

Joyful Parent = Happy Home

Copyright © 2015 by Mary Hudson

ISBN 13: 978-160683-996-6

Visit the author's website at www.keithhudson.org.

Published by Harrison House Publishers

Tulsa, OK www.harrisonhouse.com

Contents

Foreword by Jentezen Franklin

Introduction

1 Joy Is Your Strength 11

2 Relentless Love 21

3 These Are Not Your Daughter's Jeans 31

4 Believe God for the Victory 39

5 A Choice to Rejoice 51

6 Get Refocused 57

7 Moving Toward the Light 69

8 Shout It Out 77

9 The Power of the Anointing 89

10 Start Talking Right 99

11 Shake It Off 111

12 Joy Defeats Darkness 119

13 Reap in Joy 131

14 Rest and Rejoice 141

15 Wait on the Lord 161

Appendix A: Scriptures to Pray Over Your Children 169

Appendix B: Prayer of Salvation 179

Notes

DEDICATION

Thank God for His faithfulness to see us through this project. His Holy Spirit is always there to bring us joy

This book is dedicated to all parents who are looking for their children to fulfill their calling according to their "individual gift or bent;" parents who are ready to change their attitude and look up to Him and not down at the circumstances. God has a whole new view for you from the top!

FOREWORD

THE FIRST TIME we met Mary Hudson, my wife and I knew she was a special mother. In a casual conversation she made a statement that touched us to our core: "You will never win your children to Christ if you are a joyless parent."

Let's face it: children don't always do what they are supposed to do. At one time we all rebelled against God's ways. But our heavenly Father never abandoned us, and He never instructed us to reject those who do not conform to our personal standards of righteousness.

As hard as it may be to watch your children make choices that don't line up with God's Word, it's never wrong to love your kids. You are never compromising when you love. You are never lowering the standard when you love. Love says to your children—gay or straight, right or wrong, doing good or doing bad—"You're mine for the rest of your life. I will love you no matter what."

Your children need your hugs. They need your kind words. They need your influence in their lives.

Mary Hudson taught me that God never gives us permission to be mean and angry to our loved ones when they're not living for Christ. Love says, "I may not agree with your lifestyle, but I love you." It says, "You may not be doing what I approve of, but you're mine. As long as I am alive, I will love you. You can't make me not love you. You can't kick me out of your life. I want to eat with you. I want to talk with you on the phone. I want a relationship with you because I love you."

God calls us to love our kids like that because that's how He loves us. His love never fails. (See 1 Corinthians 13:8.)

The body of Christ is full of parents who are estranged from their children. I've heard so many heartbreaking stories. Parents say, "We just don't get along." "They live across town, but we never talk." "I've never even seen my grandchildren." This isn't what God wants for His people. We need to put our families back together.

In this great book, *Joyful Mother*, Mary will encourage you to love your way into your kids' world. She will show you how, as a parent, you can look past your hurt and love your children despite their actions. She will teach you the power of being a joyful parent and help you rediscover that love truly never fails.

—JENTEZEN FRANKLIN

SENIOR PASTOR, FREE CHAPEL

GAINESVILLE, GEORGIA

INTRODUCTION

THE FIRST TIME I encountered the Lord, it was in the last place I ever thought I would find Him. The year was 1979, and I was a radio news director in Las Vegas. Each month President Jimmy Carter invited members of the media to visit the White House to give them an inside view of government, and this particular month I had been invited to join the press corps.

Having access to the center of the most powerful government in the world was like being in the middle of a surreal whirlwind. I toured the White House and conducted a full day of interviews with the President and his cabinet, including his national security adviser, Zbigniew Brzezinski. It was pretty heady stuff for a young reporter.

As if that weren't enough to boggle my young and impressionable mind, the next day I was due to go to New York City to interview with the head of CBS Morning News. My brother, Frank Perry, was an Oscar-nominated film director and had arranged this rare opportunity for me at what was then the most powerful news outlet in the world. It was thrilling just to think about how these meetings could radically affect my life. As I stepped onto the commuter train going from Washington DC to New York City, I had no idea God had something even more amazing in store for me before I ever reached the city.

While I was sitting there on the train, all of a sudden the Lord appeared right in front of me in a pure white flowing robe, radiant with love, His glory all around Him. He spoke only one sentence, but His words burned in my heart then as they do today. His words were, "I am more powerful than any of this."

As His image faded softly into the background, I realized He was drawing a line for me between living a natural or a supernatural life. Although I was traveling between two of the most powerful cities on the globe at the time, the Lord was making it clear to me that His power is so much greater than anything the world has to offer. He is the Creator of all, and everything is subject to Him. I knew I had a choice with my life at that very moment: I could simply endure a day-to-day grind or pursue His presence and experience fullness of joy.

As you read this book, I believe you will realize that whatever you are going through right now is a drop in the bucket in the light of eternity. No matter how difficult your journey may be, you cannot stand still in the middle of it, frozen with fear; you have to keep moving through it. You accomplish that by enjoying the journey or by crying and struggling all the way, your choice. When you focus on how bad your problems are, they become bigger than the answers Jesus Christ died to give you. The only way to get your mind off the situation at hand and onto your answer is by focusing on the answer, His Word, and your real source of strength: His joy. What do you do when your football team wins the game? You don't get down and weep and cry and moan. You get up and cheer and hoop and holler! Likewise, God won your victory by sending Jesus to the cross 2000 years ago. Now it is time for us to accept the victory He wrought for us. If you believe you have that victory, your face will show it. At times when we are on the platform ministring, we look out over the congregation. We see some people that look like they have "lost their best friend and their dog." These Christians have lost their joy and the victory along with it. But this is the day of restoration. Changing your attitude and your perspective in the midst of a bad situation will lift you up and out..

I know this from experience. After walking through one of the most difficult days I ever faced as a parent, I became so shaken that I ended up in an extremely dark place. For several months, depression surrounded me like a wet blanket. It was a challenge to get through everyday life. Then one morning I opened my Bible to Psalm 113:9, amp. "He makes the barren woman ... a joyful mother of [spiritual] children." The words seemed to jump into my heart..

As I read that verse, the Lord was revealing that if I wanted my children to be spiritual, I had to change my attitude and rejoice as never before. Instead of wallowing over the situation, I had to thank Him in advance for what He was going to do in my family. Adjusting my attitude radically changed my perspective—and as I did that, the situation started to change. It had nothing to do with my children but everything to do with me.

As you read this book, my hope is that you will start to see there is a different way of looking at your family. You don't have to be stuck in a dark place when the Lord wants you to get up and start walking in the light. The Bible says, "Everything was created through him; nothing—not one thing!—came into being without him. What came into existence was Life, and the Life was Light to live by. The Life-Light blazed out of the darkness; the darkness couldn't put it out" (John 1:3–5, THE MESSAGE).

The light *will* overcome the darkness. God has a great life waiting for you and your family. Just follow Him, stand on His Word, and start to get happy. Especially when you don't feel like it....

CHAPTER 1

Joy Is Your Strength

You may have seen the animated musical film *Happy Feet*. As the story goes, the emperor penguin Mumble is born into a tribe of penguins. The only way these birds from Antartica can find their soul mates is by singing a "heartsong." If the male penguin's song matches the female's, the two penguins have found their mate. But the star of the show, Mumble, is born with a huge social disability: he can't sing. He does have one amazing talent, however. He can tap dance! Unfortunately this is a talent no other penguin in his tribe has ever encountered so Mumble is immediately scorned by his own clan. Instead of living in defeat and discouragement, Mumble makes a choice to rejoice. He finds a another group of penguins who accept his outlandish style of courtship. He eventually comes back to his tribe and dances his way to the penguin wife of his dreams.

This is the choice parents get to make when a family situation seems to go off course. First of all, don't get defeated by rejection, but make a choice to rejoice, no matter what your situation looks like. You can either stay down and under the situation, or you can look at it as an overcomer. Make a decision to dance your way to a place of joy and victory. Also find people who are in a worse situation than you are and plant seeds of hope into their lives. God wants you to praise Him in advance for breakthrough in your family.

We see many times in Scripture that God sends the victory *after* His people thank Him. He wants to see if you really believe His word before the evidence shows up. That is raw, undiluted faith. When Paul and Silas were beaten and thrown into a putrid dungeon with a death sentence scheduled at dawn, their joy precipitated their breakthrough. These disciples decided to exercise the power of praise in the middle of a life-threatening situation. Even though they had done nothing wrong, they didn't get angry or embittered; they raised their voices in song. This was not a natural response, because they had nothing to be happy about. And neither will yours feel natural when you first start walk into it. But that is the big dividing line between choosing to "stand on the word" or be swayed by your feelings, which are constantly changing.

Think about the results though: Not only did this supernatural attitude get Paul and Silas released from jail, but it also resulted in their jailer's getting saved with his whole household.. More people will get born again when Christians show the joy of their salvation.

I remember seeing Christians before I asked the Lord into my heart, and I could not figure out why they looked so happy. As a journalist, I came to the conclusion it must be fake. These Christians must have been putting this on. After all I had been raised in a denominational church and none of them were ever happy. But once the Lord came into my heart, I became the same way! The old saying goes, "You can stand in a garage but that doesn't' make you a car." Just because you go to church doesn't insure that you have a relationship with God. Asking Him into your heart is what makes your spirit come alive and you are become released from guilt and shame. Whom the Son sets free is free indeed. Life became fresh and new with this new birth.

If your children decide to follow a different path, that's not the time to throw in the towel and give up, although many parents definitely feel like it. Actually, this can be the beginning of a great opportunity. There is no testimony without a test. Joy is a vital weapon in your spiritual arsenal. It is the bridge between the "amen" of your prayer and the "there it is" of your answer. Praise is what you do while you're standing on God's Word, waiting for Him to bring the victory. If you just stand there like a stick, there is no life in those prayers. You have to show Him that you believe you receive the answer at the moment you pray, not when that child comes running back into your arms. That is the faith that pleases God, not the Thomas kind of faith that says "I will believe it when I see it."

Turn those days of waiting into days of worship. Don't wonder why, just praise Him and remind Him of His promises. "But You promised, God..." It isn't you making up Acts 16:32 that says you and all your household shall be saved. It is a Biblical truth that has stood the test of 2000 years of Christian prayers.

I had been on my knees for days and yet was drawing a blank. It was a hard situation. I had always expected things would turn out one way, yet they were going ninety-to-nothing in the other direction. I was consumed with guilt, blaming myself and allowing the enemy to bombard my thought life with reasons why this had happened. Then out of the blue one morning, the Lord quickened me with that scripture, Psalm 113:9, and spoke to me, "He makes the barren woman . . .to be a joyful mother of [spiritual] children." The light of revelation started to go off in me, like a "smart bomb" of Scripture, immediately calming my emotions. This fresh *rhema* word restored my peace in an instant, once I realized what He was saying to me. The Bible is alive with God and His person, just waiting to speak to your heart. There is a fresh word for you, too, if you will search for it.

You may have been in exactly the same place. You have stood for one or more of your children in some area, but there is no visible change. When the Lord took me to that scripture, He showed me what was missing. I needed to get happy before there was anything to be happy about. My bad perspective on this situation was taking me in the opposite direction of where I wanted to go. Instead of changing things for the better, I was only creating a wedge of division and making matters worse. Was I going to believe what I saw or what He said?

I know how difficult it can be to watch your children do things "their way," especially when it looks like it is totally the opposite of God's way. You want to shout, "Stop!" because you clearly see the danger ahead. But whether your children are adults or still living at home, if they are away from the Lord, standing in the gap through prayer and continually thanking God in advance for the victory is the primary way you will see them return. Your child may not be open to your advice, your relationship may be strained, or you may not be speaking at all. But as you seek Him first, God's Spirit will start to flow through you and touch your son or daughter. Your offspring is foraging through a minefield of demonic influences in this fallen world. Your prayers make all the difference to their ability to overcome.

Instead of just telling your children they are making wrong choices, you have to appeal to the Source. My father used to say to me, "Always go to the top." That is what we as parents have to do if we want to see change in our children. The Bible says, "Trust God from the bottom of your heart; don't try to figure out everything on your own. Listen for God's voice in everything you do, everywhere you go" Proverbs 3:5, THE Msg. We enter His throne room boldly and plead our case before the Lord. After all, He is the One who tells us, "Believe on the Lord Jesus Christ, and thou shalt be saved, *and thy house*" (Acts 16:31, KJV, emphasis added).

Many Christians live in ignorance of what they possess as a result of Jesus's sacrifice at Calvary. When a relative leaves you an inheritance in a will, the money is yours. It is written in a contract sealed by that person's passing. The only thing that delays you receiving that inheritance is the legal process.

Likewise, Jesus established a new covenant with His death, burial, and resurrection. That is your birthright as a believer. You can depend on what God has promised in His Word—and praise God in advance for the victory, no matter how bad the situation looks. It belongs to you but you have to claim it. A 2011 Time Magazine article claims there is more than 30 billion dollars of unclaimed money in the US alone. How many unclaimed promises are there out there for you?

The purpose of this book is to provoke you into action. When we worship God before we see change, our attitude turns from one of judgment and despair to one of joy and thankfulness. The Bible promises us He will turn our sorrow into joy:

Hear this, nations! GOD's Message! Broadcast this all over the world! Tell them, "The One who scattered Israel will gather them together again. From now on he'll keep a careful eye on them, like a shepherd with his flock." I, GOD, will pay a stiff ransom price for Jacob; I'll free him from the grip of the Babylonian bully. The people will climb up Zion's slopes shouting with joy, their faces beaming because of GOD's bounty— Grain and wine and oil, flocks of sheep, herds of cattle. Their lives will be like a well-watered garden, never again left to dry up. Young women will dance and be happy, young men and old men will join in. I'll convert their weeping into laughter, lavishing comfort, invading their grief with joy. I'll make sure that their priests get three square meals a day and that my people have more than enough. GOD's Decree.

Again, GOD's Message: "Listen to this! Laments coming out of Ramah, wild and bitter weeping. It's Rachel weeping for her children, Rachel refusing all solace. Her children are gone, gone—long gone into exile." But GOD says, "Stop your incessant weeping, hold back your tears. Collect wages from your grief work." GOD'S Decree. "They'll be coming back home! There's hope for your children." GOD'S Decree.

JEREMIAH 31:13–17, MSG

Your children will return from the land of the enemy. God has not forgotten your child.

God's plans for your children are not annulled because they have taken a different path. When you start meditating on scriptures like these, they act like mine sweepers against the negative thoughts the enemy is throwing at you. You will lose the defeatist attitude that makes you feel like your prayers never get answered.

When you stand strong on the truth of God's Word and declare His promises over your children, you will begin to see change. No matter how the situation looks in the natural.

In 2 Chronicles 20, King Jehoshaphat sent the praisers out into battle before Israel's army. The Bible says, "When they began to sing and to praise, the Lord set ambushments against the men of Ammon, Moab, and Mount Seir who had come against Judah, and they were [self-] slaughtered" (v. 22). In other words, the enemies turned on each other!

Praise is an offensive weapon, not just something you do at the end of a prayer. It is actually one of the most effective tools in your prayer arsenal. As Nehemiah 8:10 says, the joy of the Lord is our strength—both His joy over us and our joy in Him. This verse is an actual recipe for victory in the Christian life. Joy is what gives you the fortitude to endure trials and temptations you normally would give up on; it is what takes you from saying a prayer to having the answer.

Once you figure out what is stealing your joy, you have won half the battle! Think about what you go through and your reactions to people in your everyday life. What are you allowing or WHO are you letting upset you? You are letting someone have power over you, to control you emotionally, to "Hold your 'Happy' Hostage" as a friend of mine once preached. After all, strife does not going to improve your relationship, it will only divide it. The key here is to find your peace and keep your lines of communication open. Let His peace umpire your thought life (and especially what you say, the by-product of your thoughts …) before you do say anything. If a policeman directs you to cross the road and you just sit at the crosswalk ignoring him, you will not get anywhere and probably will make a lot of drivers behind you irritated.

Depression doesn't make anything happen. It actually keeps you from pressing into God. Webster's Dictionary defines *depression* as "sadness, inactivity, difficulty in thinking and concentration, a significant increase or decrease in appetite and time spent sleeping, feelings of dejection and hopelessness, and sometimes suicidal tendencies."[1] What a roadblock to trusting God for family breakthrough!

In the fifties, there was a minister's wife who was so depressed, she could hardly come out of her bedroom for over a year. Even though she had a family to raise, her mental state was such that she just could not cope.. Then one day, her husband started reading scriptures to her about who she was in Christ from a minibook by Kenneth Hagin. Her spirit started to stand up on the inside and she realized that she, as a child of the Most High, did not have to live under a cloud of depression. This dear lady years later was known for her irrepressable joy. Sometimes in the middle of her husband's message, she would spontaneously get up and run around the church when something he said sparked her to get happy. Others in the congregation would get up and run after her. Her joy was contagious. You can still see that today in some churches where a preacher says something that causes people to rise up out of their seats and take off running. As the old saying goes, 'they hit a gusher.' All three of her sons are now serving in full time ministry, while she has moved to heaven and is definitely having a party up there among the great cloud of witnesses.

God wants you to take ownership of the fact that "in thy [God's] presence is *fulness* of joy; at thy right hand there are pleasures for evermore" (Psalm 16:11, KJV, emphasis added). Many Christians mistakenly believe they have to deprive themselves of pleasure like a Medieval monk and live an ascetic life until their prayer is answered. Nothing could be further from the truth. After you have prayed, a thankful attitude is proof that you believe God, no matter what you see.

Answered prayer is supposed to be one of the ongoing sources of our happiness. The Bible says, "If ye abide in me, and my words abide in you, ye shall ask what ye will, and it shall be done unto you ... These things have I spoken unto you, that my joy might remain in you, and that your joy might be full" (John 15:7, 11, KJV).

Praise is the vital ingredient that pushes the answer through. In fact, I submit to you that unless you do thank God *in advance*, your breakthrough will be blocked. Praise is an act of faith for sure, but putting more of it on your scales balances out unbelief and doubt every time.

The case for joy in this dark age could not be clearer. We are seeing earthquakes, tornadoes, and tsunamis in places where such events have never occurred before. It is obvious that Christ's coming is drawing near. But are you to be frozen in fear for your loved ones? No! It's time to reinforce the rebar of your faith by rising up with simple, childlike praise. It is time to realign your thinking. Negative, tormenting thoughts that say your children will never come to faith will die in the face of praise.

CHAPTER 2

Relentless Love

IF YOU WANT to see your children turn back to God, a big dose of unconditional love is another primary ingredient make that dream rise. Moping around the house and becoming depressed because of the choices your children make, creates an atmosphere that may be the blockade keeping them away from God. Even if you are careful not to criticize their choices, even if you're praying in faith for them to return to the Lord, if your words are not combined with nonjudgmental affection, your prayers will be short-circuited.

When your children are in a wayward state, you may be the only Bible they read. And trust me, they are watching you like a hawk, no matter what they say! They know if you are really walking in love. When you allow God's love to manifest in your life, you present the greatest incentive to your children to return to the Lord.

Your children are looking for someone who will love them unconditionally. If you criticize and condemn your offspring without showing them genuine love, they will look for someone else who will take an interest in them. And often they look for this affection in all the wrong places.

I know this may be hard to hear, but many times the person who needs to change first is you. Your judging, haranguing, and wailing does not move anyone, except to move them away from you. The love of God is the only thing that draws a person to repentance. You have to refuse to let your feelings decide what you are going to say and do in testy situations.

Years ago I read a story that is a great example of what I am talking about. A woman walked up to Bible teacher Kenneth Hagin Jr. at one of his crusades. This lady was at her wit's end with her fifteen-year-old son. She was a new believer and had nagged him into oblivion about giving his life to the Lord, but he was just getting worse. Her words were driving him further and further away. In desperation, she sought out this minister as a last resort.

Sometimes we don't see the forest for the trees when we are seeking an answer to our problems, but another person can clearly identify our solution. That's why it is a good idea to find someone who has had success in the areas you're struggling in. Very often that person can shed some light on what you are going through. A lot of times you see only part of the problem—and through an emotionally filtered lens at that—when God sees the whole picture, and He knows who can help you get a better perspective on the situation.

As parents, we can easily let our thoughts back us into a corner. Many times we think the worst about the situation, fearing our children will hurt themselves if they are not living for God. We worry about the people they connect with and the life-changing decisions they may make. We may not be able to figure out what we're doing wrong or what we should do next. Our feelings can freeze us up like a fly in an ice cube. But there is a way to thaw out and start moving again.

The woman who approached Brother Hagin was in a desperate place. She feared her son might go to jail, get into a car accident, or something even worse. Her fears had her in a nervous frenzy. Everything she imagined was negative, but she believed this minister would have an answer for her. She walked up to this preacher and asked him to promise her something.

"Well, what is it? I'm not going to promise until you tell me what it is," Brother Hagin said.

The woman started to cry and said she was a widow with a fifteen-year-old son who was running wild. She had accepted Christ only three years before, so her son hadn't been raised in church. He had begun to abuse drugs and frequently would stay out until three or four in the morning. His mother didn't know what to do and would just lie in bed waiting for the police to call and say he had been arrested. So she begged Brother Hagin, "Promise me that you'll pray for him every day." This woman was expecting a disaster, and if she had waited long enough, it surely would have materialized. Satan is more than willing to meet our negative expectations.

Brother Hagin replied, "I'm not going to do it! I'm not going to make a promise like that because from all probability, I'd never remember to pray for him every day."

The woman pleaded, "Well, then just pray for him when it comes to you."

Hagin said, "I'm not even going to pray for him at all. It wouldn't do any good for me to pray for him as long as you keep on going the way you're going."

The woman asked, "What do you mean?"

He went on to explain that as long as the woman continually criticized and condemned her son, he would just resent her, and she might turn him off to Jesus altogether. Brother Hagin asked the woman to promise him something instead. He asked her to just leave her son alone. Instead of constantly saying he would end up in jail and nagging him about going to church or reading the Bible, he wanted her to just walk in love toward him. And at night, instead of worrying, he told her to say, "I surround him with faith and love. I don't believe he's going to wind up in jail. I believe he's going to serve God." In other words, instead of believing the worst about the boy, she needed to speak God's will and His Word, and she needed to put action to her faith by walking in love toward him.

The mother promised to do what Brother Hagin said. About fifteen months later, Brother Hagin was in the same area teaching, and a woman came up to him after the service. She asked, "Do you remember me?"

Brother Hagin didn't remember the woman until she began to tell him the story of how she asked him to pray for her son every day. He didn't recognize her because she looked much younger and prettier. The woman told Brother Hagin she went home and did just what he told her to do. "And do you know what," she asked.

"What?" Hagin asked.

"About six months ago, my son came home at four o'clock in the morning on a Saturday night. Well, I got up that morning when I usually do and started fixing breakfast because I was going to Sunday school and church. My son got up and ate breakfast with me and said, 'Mom, I believe I'll go with you to Sunday school and church this morning.'

"On the inside of me something was turning flips. But on the outside, I just said, 'Now, son, you didn't get in until late. You need your rest. You've got to go to school tomorrow.'

"'No,' he said. 'I want to go.'

"I just acted like I didn't care if he went to church with me or not. But he did go to church with me. The next Saturday night, the same thing happened. He got in about four o'clock. But the next morning he got up and ate breakfast with me. Then he said, 'Mom, I believe I'll go to Sunday school and church with you this morning.'

"I told him, 'But son, you need your rest. You've got to go to school tomorrow.'

"'No,' he said, 'I want to go.' So he went. Then that same Sunday night he said, 'I believe I'll go to church with you tonight.' He went to church that night, and when the altar call was given, he went to the altar and got saved.

"You know, before he was saved, he was 100 percent for the devil. But now that he's born again, he's 120 percent for God. I believe he's going to turn into a preacher! I'm so glad I've got a brand-new boy! Not only have I got a brand-new boy, but he's got a brand-new momma!"

The woman told Brother Hagin she didn't worry about her son anymore. "I learned how to pray in faith and walk in love," she said. "Sometimes I almost have to pinch myself and say, 'Is this really you?,' because I think so differently now."[1]

This woman got a brand-new son when she decided to appropriate a brand-new attitude. This woman saw the situation with her son from one angle, but she had not considered God's point of view at all. She was trying to change her son with a religious attitude and had forgotten about the importance of reestablishing their relationship.

Granted, it was not easy for her to change, and it will not be easy for you either. But, like anything else, if you keep at it, you will see your children respond to the love you show. Persistence brings answered prayer.

When I traded depression for joy, I gained a whole new perspective. As I began to find strength by spending time in God's presence, I felt the Father's heart, which was a heart of extravagant, unconditional love. I realized that is how I must love my children— extravagantly and unconditionally.

I know it can be difficult to not criticize your child's choices when they are unhealthy and ungodly. But speaking negative words such as, "Son, you will never amount to anything!" or "Child, you will be the death of me yet," never produces good fruit. Words are powerful vessels; they are containers of the products of our hearts. Sometimes we speak things by rote, things we just grew up hearing. They don't mean a lot to us when we are saying them.

They're just something to end an argument or express frustration. But these careless statements can go down into the deep recesses of a child's heart and come back up at the worst times, when they are lonely, sad, or about to do something self-destructive such as cutting, abusing drugs or alcohol, or worse.

Proverbs 18:21 says life and death are in the power of the tongue. That is not some vague platitude from another age. God's Word is alive and full of power for today, right now. It pays for us as parents to guard our mouths, as frustrating as the situations we face with our children can be. We must speak words of wisdom as often as they will be received. We have to encourage our children with a vision for their future, with the plans the Lord has for them. We need to remind them that the world will use and abuse them, but God will never fail them.

When we judge and criticize others, even those in our own family whom we may think we have a "right" to condemn, we are just opening a door to bring all that judgment and criticism back on ourselves. The Bible makes this clear.

Don't pick on people, jump on their failures, criticize their faults—unless, of course, you want the same treatment. That critical spirit has a way of boomeranging. It's easy to see a smudge on your neighbor's face and be oblivious to the ugly sneer on your own. Do you have the nerve to say, "Let me wash your face for you," when your own face is distorted by contempt? It's this whole traveling road-show mentality all over again, playing a holier-than-thou part instead of just living your part. Wipe that ugly sneer off your own face, and you might be fit to offer a washcloth to your neighbor.

—MATTHEW 7:1–5, THE MESSAGE

The enemy wants you to waste your time worrying about everyone's shortcomings except your own. That way you'll never take inventory of your own faults. People will spot your hypocrisy a mile away. God is the only one who can change someone. We can't even change ourselves (*phew*, what a relief!), but we can let the Holy Spirit rearrange our hearts as we hear and obey His promptings. When He has finished His work in us, we will be fit to help other people, including our own children, out of a heart filled with love and humility.

Our children need to know we honor and respect them no matter what they are doing, and we must be there for them when they need us. If you know you have been judgmental toward your children and have not been there for them when they needed you, just humble yourself and go to them and say you are sorry. That might seem off the wall when the shoe looks like it is on the other foot. But when you open a door to lay your heart before them, it willcome back to bless you. Humility is not beating yourself up over your mistakes. It is actually being open to the perfect will of God. Think about where you were and what you were doing before you committed your life to God.

If your child is involved in things you don't allow in your house, you have to set boundaries. Let them know that if they do A, then B is the consequence. But if they are out of the house, making their own decisions, then that is a different situation, where you walk on a highway of praise, believing an answer that you do not yet see, and relying on your Heavenly Father to do the work..

We can't condemn young adults after they leave home. We have to demonstrate God's unconditional love.. We don't have to condone ugly behavior, but we can let our children know our love for them does not change. Extending unconditional love draws them nearer to us—and to Him.

Joyful Parent

CHAPTER 3

These Are Not Your daughter's Jeans

THIS GENERATION IS in the middle of a cultural Armageddon. Teenagers and young adults are constantly being assaulted with immoral and often perverted messages from movies, television, music, and the Internet. On a simple trip to the mall, girls are presented with life-sized photos of partially undressed men in the most popular department stores. Our boys are fed a constant diet of racy commercials and violent, sexually explicit video games.

Satan's visual attack on our youth is relentless, and they can't fight him alone. Parents and grandparents must take to their prayer closet and walk in their God-given authority. If not, the enemy is waiting to devour a generation. Consider this: correctional facilities are one of the fastest growing industries in the United States. The number of jail inmates increased more than 9 percent since 2000 and is expected to rise another 7.5 percent by 2016.[1]

Research has shown time and again that young men raised without fathers make up the majority of the prison population. Clearly there is a cry for men and women who will stand in the gap for this generation. Children can't be left to raise themselves. Most people know this intuitively. Mothers, do you remember the sense of responsibility that dawned on you the moment you knew you were expecting your first child? All of a sudden, life no longer revolved around you. Now you were making decisions for another human being. You wondered, "Will it be bad for the baby if I drink alcohol or caffeine, take prescription drugs, or exercise too much or too little?" The unborn child growing daily in your womb suddenly took precedence above everything else in your life. You started a whole new era in your walk with God: praying for your unborn baby and his future.

That burden to nurture and protect your children and guide them spiritually does not change as they age. But when our children become adults, they must make their own decisions about whether they are going to follow God. It is not up to us. The Lord did not create us to play the role of the Holy Spirit in our children's lives or anyone else's. We are not Holy Ghost, Jr. We have to rest in the fact that we trained our children up in the way they should go, and even if they stray, they will return. (Proverbs 22:6).

Our children will explore the world on their own, make their own choices, and sometimes, unfortunately, make mistakes like we did at their age. That is one of the ways we learn how to live life—by experiencing its pitfalls. Of course, The Lord would rather have us take the easier way and renew our minds with His Word and make decisions that honor Him. But when we choose not to take that road, God will use peoples' prayers and non-judgmental attitude to get through to us.

It may seem impossible to believe that now, especially if your children are barely speaking to you, but in time they will realize that you were right about some things. It's like a quote often attributed to Winston Churchill: "When I was sixteen, I thought my parents knew nothing. When I was twenty-one, I was shocked to discover how much they picked up in five years." How many of us once thought the same thing? With each passing year we discover that our parents had a lot more wisdom than we gave them credit for. Our children will do the same. They may get angry with you as teenagers or young adults, but eventually they will begin to think that maybe you're right and they're wrong. Just give them time.

GUARD YOUR RELATIONSHIP

So what do you do when you see your child veering off course? Sit there and let it happen? It can often feel like the wind was knocked out of you when a child—the very one you prayed for and nurtured for so many years—seems to be heading in the wrong direction. Not only do you *not* feel like praying, but you may also want to get in the child's face and give him a piece of your mind.

That is the worst thing you can do when the devil is making a play for their souls. When children stray from what they have been taught, we can't shut them out. As I mentioned in the previous chapter, if you don't engage your children and spend time with them, they will look elsewhere for attention.

Just as they needed you to listen to them when they were young, they need you to listen to them now. The six years between the ages of twelve and eighteen are critical times for you to always be ready to hear them, no matter what they want to talk about.

The exciting part is that they are confident enough to talk to you. You want to be the one your child feels safest talking with so you can know how to pray.

That doesn't change as your children age. Lending a nonjudgmental ear, one that is there to listen and not comment, is the most effective tool you will have in drawing your child back to a closer relationship with you and Him. Some of what they tell you may be hard to hear. Take it to your prayer closet and leave it there. Even if you are alarmed by what your child tells you, one of the worst things you can do is betray that confidence by telling your friends. Trust those secrets to the heart of God.

Parents (and adults who are called to minister to young people) must create an environment that is loving, nurturing, and safe so their children will feel free to communicate with them. This may feel awkward to you if you were raised in an environment where your parents rarely talked with you. But making time to listen to your children when they need to talk and giving them your undivided attention will bring eternal rewards.

The love of God flowing through you is what will draw your children back. That is why you have to keep your relationship intact, no matter what your children are doing or how they are behaving. It is easy to get angry when your children are rebelling; it often takes great patience to not shut them off after you have expressed your opinion about how you think they should live. They are old enough to think for themselves. It is time to let them. Get angry at the enemy. He is your problem. You are not fighting flesh and blood but powers and principalities. Once you see it as spiritual warfare, it is a lot easier to be objective about it.

Your position now is to stand before God and worship Him. Many times children want to listen to their parents because they know they have wisdom that can help them. But when that parent constantly condemns, judges, or crushes the child's spirit, he will go to someone else—anyone who will have an ear open to hear his heart. Rather than speaking words that destroy, speak those that encourage. You can pray alone but also remember that your prayers with your mate or another strong believer will put ten thousand devils to flight.

Take Courage

If your child is going in what you feel is the wrong direction, it's natural for you to want to tell him all the reasons he should change—*now*! But sometimes the little side trips along the road are part of them finding out who they are and developing into what they want to be. They are the captains of their own ship after the age of 18, and they are the only ones who can decide what to do do with their lives. So you can talk to them all you want, but they have to digest and take ownership of it.

This is a spiritual battle, and you must fight for your child with superior firepower—which is God's plan of rejoicing, praising, and declaring His Word. When Paul and Silas were in prison and facing certain death at daybreak, they decided to start praising God. As a result, the Lord sent an angel to open the prison doors, and they were set free. Praising God will open the doors to your child's heart too. What you do in secret will manifest in the open.

Throughout the Bible God told His people to "be of good courage." God spoke those words to Joshua four times when he was leading the children of Israel to possess the land He had promised them. We must have courage too, as we stand in faith that God will keep His promise to us concerning our children. God knows exactly what we are going through, and He hears our prayers. He is more concerned for our children than we ever will be. The Lord knows demons have been assigned to destroy our children's future and to sabotage our joy with depression. That is why, after we as parents have prayed about the situation, we need to thank God for hearing us and for already providing the answer. This shows the Lord we believe He can do what we asked Him for in the first place. Only the Holy Spirit can reach our children no matter what they are doing. After we have prayed and praised, it is time to cast the care on Him.

Torment is a powerful tool the enemy uses against parents. I remember waking up in the middle of the night when my husband and I were ministering in a city back east. We were three thousand miles away from our home in California, and the enemy was tormenting me with fear because our children had driven to Las Vegas and were spending the night with their grandmother. My thoughts raced: *What were they going to do in Sin City? Will they be safe? Will they get themselves into trouble?* One of the children was still underage at the time. What would happen if they walked down the Las Vegas Strip and were enticed to go into the casinos? Whom would they meet? What if someone tried to take advantage of them? What if they ran into some drug dealers or prostitutes? I was a mental mess. Fear brings torment and it was staring me down at high noon.

This is how the devil works. He creates stories and plants "what-if" scenarios in our minds to get us focused on our fears instead of praying in faith for God to protect our children. I walked the floor, crying and begging God to keep my children safe. Finally my husband insisted I get back in bed and relax; he assured me all was well and that I was making much ado about nothing. I calmed down, and it turned out he was right. The next morning their grandmother called and reported that everything was fine. All they did was walk down the Las Vegas Strip and perform a pantomime on the sidewalk, acting like the characters they are.

This is exactly why it is critical we renew our minds daily. No football team ever won the championship sitting on the sidelines. Asian students take their academics very seriously and are always studying. They will study from seven in the morning and then come home and sutdy again until 11 pm at night. But their perisistence pays off and they have some of the highest math and science scores in the US. Think what would happen if you studied the Word as intensely as that. It worked for Joshua. "

> *This book of the law shall not depart out of your mouth, but you shall meditate on it day and night, that you may observe to do according to all that is written therein: for then you shall make your way prosperous, and then you shall have good success."*
>
> *Joshua 1:8*

You cannot be passive when you are under attack. You have to rise up and fight back when thoughts are swirling around your brain trying to exalt themselves against God's unchanging truth. "We destroy arguments and every lofty opinion raised against the knowledge of God, and take every thought captive to obey Christ" (2 Corinthians 10:5 ESV).

Cast thoughts of doom down in any area of life where they originate. This is a mandate to aggressively destroy strongholds that keep you worrying about your children's future. Remember the famous acronym about the word *fear*? False Evidence Appearing Real. The enemy's most effective weapon is deception. If you fall for satan's lie that your child is never going to change and will always live a certain way, you have been duped by one of the devil's oldest tricks.

But once you recognize that the enemy is a paper tiger, you can start fighting back with that instrument directly beneath your nose—your mouth. Start speaking life to your children, no matter what they are up to or what they are up against. You will start to see life arise in them. A friend said when she calmed down and started using this method with her adult child, her daughter was so shocked by her positive attitude that she asked, "Mom, has someone been coaching you?"

Yes, she had a coach—the Holy Spirit. He taught her how to love her child in a new way when she decided to rejoice and speak words of life instead of death. And the daughter totally turned around within the year and started to lead a productive life.

CHAPTER 4

Believe God for the Victory

JOSHUA IS A great example of someone who maintained the right attitude in the middle of a fight. He had to win many battles before he and the people of Israel could enter the Promised Land. The Lord repeatedly reminded Joshua to be of good courage, which probably means he had plenty of chances to waver. And he held onto his mindset.

The word *courage* means to have the mental or moral strength to persevere and withstand danger, fear, or difficulty.[1] You have to have an attitude of victory when you are facing dangerous or frightening circumstances. What if Joshua had decided he just couldn't handle the pressure of the constant battles, the men dying for the cause, and the resources drying up, so instead chose to throw in the towel and quit obeying the Lord's commands? We have all had that opportunity when the going gets tough. This Old Testament hero could have easily given up when the enemy came against him time after time. If he had yielded to defeat, the children of Israel would never have moved into the Promised Land. Actually, there was a whole generation of people with bad attitudes who never did make it into that land of promise.

God is not shocked by a cancer diagnosis, divorce papers, a foreclosure notice, or a child's rebellion. But you can't just sit back with a victim mentality and expect the Lord to change the situation without your standing up to the enemy and enforcing what Jesus already accomplished on the cross. Remember, you are not standing up to the child, you are taking authority over the devil who is trying to manipulate his life. You have to rise up, have faith in the Word, and get happy despite what you see.

There is no room for a "doubting Thomas" in a crisis situation. Your dynamic and forceful response to the situation will make all the difference. You will begin to see yourself winning the battle for your children's souls on your knees.

Consider this, even though it might be a huge pill to swallow (like those enormous vitamin C horse pills at health food stores): Jesus has already done everything it takes for your children to be reconciled to God. All they have to do is make the decision to agree with His Word and receive Him as their Savior or return to Him as their first love. You can pray for them, and that will soften their hearts, but it is up to them to move back into fellowship.. Stand on God's Word, believing Him for the victory.

Receive What Jesus Accomplished

When Jesus died on the cross two thousand years ago, He became the final sacrifice. He took with Him to the cross everyone's pain, sorrow, and rebellion, including yours! He has already finished the work to bring your child to salvation. He completed His job.

Now it is your responsibility to be proactive and use the delegated authority you have in Him. You have to rest in Him and receive what He accomplished on the cross.

Jesus was crucified so you could experience resurrection power in every area of your life. One of the first books Kenneth E Hagin ever wrote was called *In Him*. This little book explains what the Bible says about who you are in Christ and encourages you to speak that truth out loud. But you may balk at that and say, "Mary, I don't need that," or, "I'm way beyond that." But I have learned I am not beyond anything as long as my spirit is encased in flesh.

You have to understand how the Lord looks at you. He sees you as more than a conqueror, as someone who has all power over the enemy—because that's who you are. Jesus reclaimed the authority Satan stole in the Garden of Eden when mankind sinned with the resurrection power that lifted him out of the grave. Ephesians 2:6 says we are seated in heavenly places with Christ, which means we are equipped with the authority He has over Satan.

When you realize who you are in Him, you can see you are not fighting this battle on your own. You have all the resources of heaven backing you up. Think about this: What if you had all the gold at Fort Knox backing your bank account? Money would no longer be an issue. The same goes for your authority in Christ. You have all of heaven backing you as you stand on God's Word that your house will be saved.

When you consider that Jesus has already done the heavy lifting for you, start to treat your children as if they are serving God and refuse to put emphasis on what you see in everyday life. Those things are temporary; they will change. Romans 4:17 declares that God "calleth those things which be not as though they were" (KJV). You have to call the situation as the Lord sees it, not as you see it. And you have to declare the end from the beginning before you see any evidence of it.

The facts of the situation might look bad. Your children might be on drugs, abusing alcohol, or sleeping around. But their condition does not nullify God's Word. His Word will change their situation if you consistently and thoroughly apply it with your mouth, personalizing the scripture by putting your child's name in it. I have included a list of great scriptures in the appendix that will help you do this. You can pray verses such as Isaiah 28:17–18 (KJV): "And the hail shall sweep away the refuge of lies, and the waters shall overflow the hiding place. And [insert your child's name] covenant with death shall be disannulled, and [their] agreement with hell shall not stand."

God's Word is Neosporin for your wounds. The bruise will heal if you consistently apply it.

Start to realize that God has a better plan for your child's life than you, or he, thinks He has. Speak a future word about that child in your prayer life. Proverbs 22:6 says, "Train up a child in the way he should go [and in keeping with his individual gift or bent], and when he is old he will not depart from it." Every child has a particular God-given ability. If properly and consistently nurtured, encouraged, prayed over, and declared, your child will grow up to be a champion, even if there are a few bumps along the way.

Your words in prayer, calling those things that be not as though they are, turn the tide in the heavenlies in your favor. Don't allow circumstances to move you. Let the Word direct your heart into peace, and let that peace maintain your stability (Philippians 1:28).

A Light in the Darkness

Imagine waking up in the middle of the night and trying to make your way to the bathroom in the dark. You might stumble over something if you don't find a flashlight or something to light your way. So it is with dark situations. When you don't know what to do, you need the lamp of the Bible to get you over to the other side.

His Word is a book of promises breathed from God's heart to you. The Holy Spirit will personally illuminate certain phrases He wants you to use as battle weapons. You might be in the middle of conflict with your child. He may be hanging with the wrong friends, rebelling, running away, angry, engaging in prostitution, or holding on to bitterness. Whatever the circumstance, you need God's help to know the way out.

God has a solution for you if you will seek Him with all your heart. The Word promises to show you what to do, as Psalm 97:11 says, "Light is sown for the [uncompromisingly] righteous and strewn along their pathway, and joy for the upright in heart [the irrepressible joy which comes from consciousness of His favor and protection]."

When you pray the promises of God, the angels begin to war on your behalf. Psalm 103:20–21 says, "Bless the LORD, you His angels, who excel in strength, who do His word, heeding the voice of His word. Bless the LORD, all you His hosts, you ministers of His, who do His pleasure" (NKJV). Angels hearken *only* to the Word of God—not to your tears or your pleadings. When you speak God's Word aloud, you give the angels their marching orders.

There is power in the Word of God. In Matthew 8 the centurion, who was not even Jewish, knew enough about the authority of Jesus's words to say, "Speak the word only, and my servant shall be healed" (v. 8, KJV). Jesus later commended this centurion's great faith, saying, "I tell you truly, I have not found so much faith as this with anyone, even in Israel" (v. 10). In Matthew 15, Jesus also commended the faith of the Syropheonecian woman, because she knew that He needed only to say the word and her daughter would be made whole (vv. 21–28). Both were justified because they understood Jesus' authority. They knew if Jesus said something, it had to be so.

It is like a policeman who has been given orders to direct traffic at an intersection. He is not stopping cars on his own authority; he is relying on the word of his commander in chief. His boss told him what to do, and he is following his command. He knows his commander will back him up if anyone challenges him. That is the same way we use the Word of our great Commander in Chief. We exercise the authority He has given us.

When you seek God in prayer, He will give you a word to show you which step to take. It may be a verse of scripture, as it was with me when He gave me the revelation about being a joyful mother. He may speak to your heart and then confirm that word in the Scriptures. Either way, God will direct your path and guide you in every decision you need to make with your children.

STAND ON THE WORD

There were many times as a mother when I had to stand upon the Word and thank God for the outcome, regardless of how the situation looked. The birth of my oldest daughter was a miracle; she was a living example of the power of standing and rejoicing. She should have never been born.

Before I knew anything about Christianity or being a mother, I had had an abortion at the age of eighteen. People claim abortions don't affect a woman, but that was not my experience. Even though I didn't know the Lord at the time, guilt fell on me like a lead balloon after the procedure. I knew nothing about being pro-life or pro-choice at the time. But as soon as the operation was over, I could sense a void; I knew in my heart that something very precious had been taken from me.

I was a junior at the University of California at Berkeley at the time. Six months later, I was still in such a deep depression that I would wake up at ten in the morning, go to my three classes, eat a small meal, and be back in bed by four o'clock, feeling worthless, hoping to sleep away the feelings of despair. It was as if I had become the lowest form of humanity. It was hard to forgive myself for losing that child. I tried to fill the void inside me with everything I could, but nothing could blot out the stain of guilt that lingered until I accepted Jesus as Lord.

Twelve years later, when I was born again, I experienced a

time of repentance, forgiveness, redemption, and restoration. My joy was restored. The physical scars were still there, however, unbeknownst to me. Even after I was married and born again, I struggled to conceive. My husband, Keith, and I tried for three years but nothing happened. We started to think that we would never have a child. But a determination rose up in my soul. One night I spent all night at the altar of our church, alternately laughing and crying, asking God for a child. It was clear to me that night how the prophet Samuel's mother, Hannah, might have felt when she wept bitterly before the Lord, pleading for Him to remove her barrenness. Hannah, too, had not been able to have children and was being constantly mocked and ridiculed by her husband's other wife, Penniniah. (1 Samuel 1:6)

The very next day after praying at the altar, an evangelist came through the church we pastored and prayed for women who were infertile. As I stood there in that healing line, the power of God touched my body, though I was not aware of it at the time. Ten days later, we were meeting at the church again, this time fasting and praying during our monthly all-night prayer service. Feeling sick to my stomach all night long, I had to keep slipping into the church nursery to eat saltine crackers. Later that week we learned it wasn't the stomach flu at all—I was experiencing morning sickness. Our first child was on her way!!

Angela was born nine months later. A long labor ensued at the moment of birth, and the doctors decided to take her by C-section. It turned out to be a good thing. My doctor explained that the abortion fifteen years earlier left so much scar tissue around my fallopian tubes that he would have given me only a 10 percent chance of ever getting pregnant. The very fact that she even made it into the world when most of the odds were against her demonstrated the miracle working power of God.

THE WEAPONS OF OUR WARFARE

Passivity is a sure-fire recipe for defeat. But fighting back with praise that His Word is true is a weapon of victory. We can't expect the answer to just fall at our feet. There is a war going on in the heavenlies. We have to sharpen our swords and get busy.

When you are part of a sports team, you can practice only so much before the day comes when you have to actually compete against the opponent. If you never play against the other team, you never learn where their weaknesses are and how to defeat them. As parents, we need to practice defeating our enemy the devil by using the tools that He lays at our disposal. This way we are ready in season and out to rise up against him whenever he rears his ugly head. You may say, "Oh, you are making much ado about the enemy." Unfotunately he will always be watching for the chink or weak point in your armor. His purpose is to kill, steal and destroy from your life, but you have the ability to stop that. Many years ago, Kenneth Copeland was walking into his mother's house just as her prayer meeting had ended and two ladies were leaving. As he passed by them on the sidewalk, he overheard one say, "That's the first time I ever felt sorry for the devil." Apparently, the enemy had taken a serious beating in that prayer meeting.

Your children may be in bad circumstances up to their eyeballs, but nothing is impossible with God. He delights in turning seemingly hopeless situations around, just to draw the enemy into his own net—and then He gets the glory. God does the impossible for you because He loves you and your children more than you ever could, and His grace and mercy are continually being poured out on your lives.

You would be amazed if you are ever able keep a record of how many times God answered your prayers and sent people across your child's path to minister to him to speak truth that he'd never hear from you. Until you see the manifestation of the miracle of your child's salvation, you have to trust God and cast all your cares and worries into His hands. Releasing the weight of that care alone will bring you joy.

PRAISE DRAWS PEOPLE TO CHRIST

So what do you do after you've bombarded heaven and stood on every scripture you can find relating to your children? It's time to get release the weight and rejoice. Yes, you get to cast your cares on the Lord. The next step of course, is keeping your praise on. Praising and rejoicing in God are vital instruments in your arsenal if you are expecting to see answers. After all, if what you have prayed for is in accordance with God's will and His Word, and you are convinced God has heard your petition, then you do not have to be anxious about the answer. You can be at rest. You don't have to have a struggle in your mind or heart, because you know that God has everything covered, even if you see no signs of that in the natural. Just stay determined and persistent. Don't let go of what you know!!

I love to read about heroes of the faith, not only those in Scripture such as Moses and Abraham, but also those who served in the trenches of ministry on the mission field or as evangelists. John Nelson Hyde was a wonderful, partially deaf missionary in India who believed for many souls to be saved. He saw numerous missionaries begin serving in India and formed the Punjab Prayer Union in 1904. But what I like about Hyde is that he is as well known for his prayer life as he is for his work on the mission fields of India. In fact, he was nicknamed "Praying Hyde" because of his fervent commitment to prayer.

Hyde understood the importance of praise as a vital key in intercession. In a biography written about Hyde, aptly titled *Praying Hyde*, author Francis McGaw wrote about the crucial role praise played in Hyde's prayer life and in leading people to Christ.

> *I remember John telling me that in those days if on any day four souls was not brought into the fold, at night there would be such a weight on his heart that it was positively painful, and he could not eat or sleep. Then in prayer he would ask his Lord to show him what the obstacles were to this blessing. He invariably found that it was the want of praise in his life. This command, which has been repeated in God's Word hundreds of times—surely it is all important! Hyde would then confess his sin, and accept the forgiveness by the blood. Then he would ask for the spirit of praise as another gift of God. So he would exchange his ashes for Christ's garland, his mourning for*

Christ's oil of joy, his spirit of heaviness for Christ's garment of praise, and as he praised God, souls would come to him, and the numbers lacking would be made up.[2]

What McGaw is saying here is that praise was the driving force behind the results Hyde saw in prayer. Praise was not just something Hyde did during his prayer time; it was the essential key to his prayer life. And Hyde saw incredible results—thousands of souls brought into the kingdom of God. Just as metal is drawn to a magnet, so are people drawn to those with joy in their hearts and praise in their mouths and who cast their cares on the Lord and pray His promises.

CHAPTER 5

A Choice to Rejoice

I CAN'T IMAGINE IT was easy for Jesus to go to the cross. The Bible says He agonized in prayer for hours in the Garden of Gethsemane and was deeply disappointed that His disciples were too sleepy to labor with Him in prayer. But Hebrews 12:2 clearly states that Jesus endured the cross for the joy set before Him. He knew there was a purpose in the pain He was to endure, even though the prospect of being separated from the Father during those three days had to have been heartwrenching. Nevertheless on the cross Jesus declared, "Yet not My will, but [always] Yours be done" (Luke 22:42). He trusted God's way, even though it meant He would be forced to suffer. Jesus knew His sacrifice would bring salvation to the whole world. Mankind was reconciled to God that day because Jesus chose to follow His Father's plan, as agonizing as it was. Your sacrifice of praise in the middle of the battle may seem like unnecessary energy expended into thin air, but it is the sweet sound of victory.

Dodie Osteen, mother of Lakewood Church Pastor Joel Osteen in Houston, Texas, is a prime example of the power of rejoicing in God and declaring His Word in a desperate situation. She was diagnosed with terminal liver cancer and given six weeks to live, but she made a decision she would call herself healed and she was going to act like it. Every day she quoted healing scriptures, cleaned the house, and made the beds, acting as if she was healed and believing God was going to spare her life. She went out to hospitals and nursing homes, praying for those who were worse off than she was.

That was over thirty years ago. She still praises God and daily declares His Word over herself. Because God prolonged her life, she has been able to see all of her children walking with the Lord and her son, Joel, become pastor of the largest church in America.[1]

James 1:2 tells us to "consider it wholly joyful, my brethren, whenever you are enveloped in or encounter trials of any sort or fall into various temptations." This verse is not saying we should be happy because our child is on drugs, is an unwed mother, or has walked away from the Lord. It is telling us to be joyful because God is going to turn the situation around. He wants to show you that He is able to do exceedingly abundantly above all you ask or think. You are demonstrating to Him through your joyful attitude that you believe He will do it.

Has God not said it? Will He not make it good? (See Isaiah 40:20–22.) Your faith in His Word, your joy and praise showing you believe it are the sparks that ignite the fire. Without believing what God says, your thoughts might as well be wet wood on that conflagration.

I know it is hard to praise God in times of stress. But the Bible clearly says praise silences the enemy (Psalm 8:2). Whatever you are going through, the length of time you stay there depends on you changing your attitude toward the situation (James 1:2). Having a a heart full of gratitude, even when you don't feel like thanking God, changes you, causes joy to rise up and gives you strength.

Dance Like David

King David literally put his marriage and family on the line when he took off his coat and praised the Lord with all his might in his underwear. (2 Samuel 6:14.) David's wife Michal despised his open act of worship to the Lord. But the king was so overwhelmed with thankfulness that the ark of the covenant—the literal presence of God—was finally being returned to its rightful place at the temple in Jerusalem, he didn't care. King David was more concerned about the opinion of the Lord rather than man's.

This sort of worship always brings God's favor. But David's wife was consumed with pride. What would her critical, gossiping friends think of her husband, the king, rejoicing in his underwear in front of the whole city? Michal was more worried about what the people around thought of her than what God thought. That was a bad call for her. Because she despised David's passionate praise, she was stricken with barrenness. Michal's haughty attitude robbed her of the opportunity to have children. Barrenness is a high price to pay for bitterness and pride.

In life, we choose our attitudes and thought patterns, whether we are consciously aware of it or not. When contradictory circumstances defy the dreams we have for our children, we choose whether we are going to agree with what we see, or make a decision to believe God's Word, release the situation to Him, and rejoice.

As I stated earlier, Jesus endured the cross for the "joy that was set before Him." Being mocked and tortured during His trial and crucifixion was a terrible ordeal for Him, but He knew what was waiting in the wings—joy that would last for eternity, much longer than His "temporary affliction." We need to look at these things we're experiencing as fleeting, because they are. What the Lord does is eternal; what people do here on earth is temporary. People in this natural realm are always subject to change while God is not.

We are in a battle for souls, and that is not something to take lightly. I know it is not always easy to rejoice in the middle of trying circumstances, but it is possible. You can start by being thankful that you are still alive and saved. We can't just sit back and say, "God will do it for me." We have to be on the offensive to see the breakthrough we're believing for.

The Lord inhabits the praises of His people. No devil in hell can permanently stop the answer from manifesting. The day of breakthrough will come. In Daniel 10, the angel essentially told the prophet Daniel, "I heard your prayer the first day you prayed, but it took twenty-one days to fight it out through the second heaven." This is the territory in the heavens where demons attempt to hinder the prayers of the saints. In that realm, your determination in prayer helps to push the answer through.

What you become conscious of, you are more empowered

to release. As a Christian, you have a ministry of releasing God's presence into the earth, and in His presence is fullness of joy. So if you are rejoicing, thankful, and happy in your daily life, looking to the Lord for your provision and direction, you will be more open to receive all the things the Lord wants to bring to you. As you expose your heart to His open heaven, you will find yourself flowing in a river of peace instead of drowning in your sorrows, especially if you are seeking first His kingdom and looking for others to help who are hurting worse than you are.

When we worship something, we put that thing first; we mark it as worthy of our praise. You don't want to make depression bigger in your life than God, do you? Of course not! So when you feel despair creep up on you make a decision to ditch that depression and get up and dance like David did.

Joyful Parent

CHAPTER 6

Get Refocused

THE ENEMY LOVES it when we act like a victim because he knows it robs us of power. If we decide we are defeated, then we have fallen right into his trap. You do not have to agree with anything the devil tells you but when you do take this tack, the devil knows he does not have to bother tormenting you anymore because you have walked right into his plan.

However, when you wake up every morning and start to rejoice before the Lord—despite the fact that your children aren't where they should be or your marriage is in trouble or you can't seem to get ahead financially—you are destroying his plan against you. Keep up the good work, and you will see results. The enemy is persistent, but he will eventually back off once he sees you peristently praising God and resting in His presence. The devil will see he's wasting his time.

Of course, staying in that place of rest and praise is the hard part. The enemy will use anything he can, especially the people closest to you, to keep you from believing. So you have to be aware of his sudden attacks. He will throw emotional fly balls out of left field, but you have to maintain your position in God's presence.

Yes, there will be people who will laugh at you for praising the Lord when your children are on drugs, in prison, alcoholic, or just away from God. But that is when you have to stand tall and start to rejoice all over again. You and the Lord will always get the last laugh, because you both know the end result.

YOU CAN CHANGE IF YOU WANT TO

If you live a life of regret and sorrow, you will find yourself in a place of spiritual barrenness. This emptiness affects everyone close to you, especially your family. After all, who wants to be around a person who is constantly depressed and forlorn? The odd part about it is, it's difficult to recognize this hole in your soul because you are so close to it. You are myopic when you are walking in it. You are so close to it, you don't see the forest for the trees. The good news is that you do not have to stay that way. You can change if you want to.

When you spend time developing a relationship with God and abiding in His presence where there is "fullness of joy ... [and] pleasures forevermore" (Psalm 16:11), you put yourself in the middle of a continual feast. You can break out of a faith famine any time you want when you make the choice to turn from darkness to light and look to God instead of your problems. What you are really doing is refocusing, choosing to believe Him instead of what stands right in front of you. That situation is always subject to change, but the Lord never changes.

I would rather gaze on God's face any day. Think about a

kaleidoscope and how many patterns it can create with just a twist of the tube. Your mind is like that. Whatever you put into it, however you think about a situation, will create a whole new map of your world as you roll it over in your mind.

Depression magnifies the enemy and gives him greater access into your life. But joy releases you to see things God's way. There are definitely downer situations in life, but there are also uppers! The psalmist in Psalm 3:3 says that despite the depressing situation he found himself in, he would not despair because "You, O Lord, are a shield for me, my glory, and the lifter of my head." His confidence was in God. He did not focus on everything around him that seemed to be falling apart.

When you are depressed, you lose strength; you weak because you are looking at your problem instead of the Lord. Make a decision today to look up and consider the possibilities, not the problems, in people around you. Trust Him to lead you into an even better situation—because He has one waiting for you. He has a plan you could have never imagined yourself, something bigger and better than you could have ever dreamed. So the key here is to lay every depressing thought at His feet. Cast the care on the Lord and let Him take it.

Dr. David Yonggi Cho, who for many years was pastor of the largest church in the world, Yoido Full Gospel Church in Seoul, Korea, tells a story in his book *The Fourth Dimension* about a woman who came to see him in great distress. She explained that though her daughter was raised as a Christian, she was living the life of a prostitute and sleeping with every man who came across her path. The daughter's lifestyle had caused her family so much distress, the woman's sons were about to leave home.

This mother explained her woeful situation to Dr. Cho, who calmly responded, "Have you considered how Jesus sees your daughter?"

The woman narrowed her eyebrows thoughtfully and said, "Well, He probably sees her saved, healed, and delivered."

Dr. Cho responded, "That is how you need to see her."

The two prayed and agreed together that this mother would get a new vision of her daughter. From that moment forward, she saw her daughter not with natural eyes but through the Spirit—the way the Lord saw her. The mother's attitude started to change in prayer. She began to thank God that her daughter was on her way back to the Lord and her family. She decided to look at the situation God's way instead of her way.

Within weeks, the daughter called crying and saying she was tired of her lifestyle and wanted to come home. This mother received her daughter with open arms. The following Sunday the daughter was in church rededicating her life to Christ.[1]

Think about the prophet Samuel's mother, Hannah. Is your situation as bad as hers? Her rival Peninnah mocked her for years because Hannah couldn't have children. But Hannah refused to whine about her raw treatment. She decided in her desperation to pour out her soul before the Lord.

And as she continued praying before the Lord, Eli noticed her mouth. Hannah was speaking in her heart; only her lips moved but her voice was not heard. So Eli thought she was drunk. Eli said to her, How long will you be intoxicated? Put wine away from you. But Hannah answered, No, my lord, I am a woman of a sorrowful spirit. I have drunk neither wine nor strong drink, but I was pouring out my soul before the Lord. Regard not your handmaid as a wicked woman; for out of my great complaint and bitter provocation I have been speaking. Then Eli said, Go in peace, and may the God of Israel grant your petition which you have asked of Him. Hannah said, Let your handmaid find grace in your sight. So [she] went her way and ate, her countenance no longer sad.

—1 SAMUEL 1:12–18

Hannah got determined and didn't let Peninnah distract her. She took her problem right to the Lord—and He answered! The child God gave her became one of the greatest prophets in the Old Testament. And after Samuel was born and was dedicated to the Lord, Hannah had other children. God turned Hannah's situation completely around because she chose not to focus on her adversary, but on the One who could bring her breakthrough.

GET AND KEEP THE RIGHT PERSPECTIVE

Some people think they can just sail along in life, as if everything is going to be handed to them on a silver platter. Then, when things don't turn out the way they thought, they wonder what happened and become despondent about the situation in front of them. The enemy can knock you down, but he cannot knock you out unless you let him.

So how do you keep from falling for his devices? It is vital to maintain an attitude of gratitude, have a heart to bless others in worse situations than your, and keep on laughing and praising, no matter what you see in the natural. How do you get and keep the right perspective?

MAKE WORSHIP A PRIORITY

Let worshiping God be the first thing you do in the morning. Thank Him for everything He is, all that He has done for you, everything you are, everything you have, your salvation, your family, and your life. You are probably not in the intensive care unit hooked up to five IVs. If you look at it that way, you have a good reason to give thanks.

DON'T COMPLAIN

Many people complain and murmur about every little thing— from the person erratically driving in the next lane to the slow person in front of them in line at the grocery store. Complaining is a language that brings death to your situation, but praising brings life. Just because the answer to your prayer is delayed does not mean it is the time to complain. And delay does not mean your answer is being denied. God may be giving you an opportunity to help someone else in the midst of your trial—to pray for someone having a hard day or someone wracked with pain, or to speak a word of encouragement to someone whose problem is worse than yours will ever be.

DON'T LEAN ON YOUR OWN STRENGTH

You can't maintain joy by leaning on your own strength. God's strength is the only thing resilient enough to sustain you when you are battling for your child's soul. And if you find it hard to pull yourself out of despair over your situation, find someone to partner with in prayer who has already had the victory in the area you are dealing with. Connect with someone who is already where you want to be, someone who has had victory with their children, who has seen them come out on the other side.

ADJUST YOUR EXPECTATION

You can get so lulled into thinking things will always be the same that you stop expecting the situation to change. If you'll let the Lord open your eyes, you'll see that God, who never changes, is bringing miracles to you on a daily basis. Your child may want to change, but because you have had the expectation for so long that "he is always going to be that way," you don't recognize his steps toward repentance when they start to manifest. Listen, we are in the last of the last days. God is going to perform some miraculous signs and wonders in these hours, and He is going to work some of those miracles in and through your children!

Psalm 22:3 says God lives in your praises. That means He is there, alive in the middle of your praises, but He cannot remain in the midst of a bad attitude. In Scripture, the Holy Spirit descended upon Jesus in the form of a dove. This bird is by nature a very sensitive creature. It will get up and fly away at the slightest disturbance. Likewise the Holy Spirit is easily grieved, which is why staying in communion with Him and being attuned to His will are vital. Think of a couple waltzing together at the refrain of the orchestra, or ice-skaters twirling on the ice in a blur of energy, perfectly choreographed. It only looks effortless because they have spent time together, developing a flow, a rhythm that keeps them in tune with each other.

GET IN GOD'S PRESENCE

You find true joy in God's presence (Psalm 21:1). Your heart is God's dwelling place, but you must open it up to His goodness, His glory, and His joy. The children of Israel knew the inner court where God dwelt was a holy place. The fear of the Lord was upon them every time they even sent a priest near that place. The high priest had to have little bells sewn on the hem of his garment because if something happened to him while he was in the inner court, which was filled with God's Shekinah glory, he would have to be pulled out. Anyone who entered that place without God's sanction would immediately drop dead.

Now that Christ has died for our sins, we as Christians are God's temple. He dwells in us, not in buildings made by man. Like the ancient temple, we have an outer court, an inner court, and a most holy place. The outer court is our physical body, the inner court is our soul, and the most holy place is our spirit. This is where the Holy Spirit dwells.

Our physical health is important, but God is much more interested in our inner life than our outer life. You need to be the same way. You need to be more concerned about what goes on inside of you, because your inner life will determine your outer behavior. A change must happen inside of you before it can happen on the outside; that is the only way you can expect to be transformed.

That is what happened when I was born again. I had to start renewing my mind with God's Word. By doing this I was able to prove for myself "what is the good and acceptable and perfect will of God" (Romans 12:2). I never would have changed my hard-hearted, cynical outer attitude after I accepted Christ in 1979 if I had not worked on my inner man by immersing myself in the Word.

As a radio news director for a Las Vegas ABC affiliate, my job was to report on the many murders and other grisly crimes uncovered daily in the deserts of Sin City. The crime reports there were enough to unsettle even the most hardened of hearts. Only by spending time studying the Word with a wonderful mentor (who later became my sister-in-law) was I able to deal with the emotional toll these assignments tried to take on me.

When I sat in front of the microphone in the studio, ready to deliver the news at the top of the hour, my voice had to be confident and unwavering, without a trace of emotion. Broadcast professionals are graded on the consistency of their voices at any given time. My station manager and coworkers (who wanted nothing to do with God at the time) would make a point of coming into my studio ten minutes before airtime and trying to belittle me about one thing or another. They were doing their best to throw me off emotionally so I couldn't deliver a quality newscast. Finally, I caught on to how the enemy was using them to steal my joy—and my job.

The telephone at my side became my lifesaver. I called my minister friend, who committed to pray with me anytime there was an attack like this. So when these coworkers began to harass me, I would quickly get on the line, and we would pray and agree together concerning a particluar verse of Scripture. After meditating on that Word, my heart was strengthened and my voice would immediately become strong and full of life. I delivered the news like a true professional and was not the on-air basket case my coworkers hoped I would turn into. Collapsing in tears would have landed me an immediate pink slip. But the joy and peace I gained by standing on Scripture gave me the courage that sustained me and caused me to overcome.

Digging into His Word will do the same for you. Thousands of thoughts race through our minds every minute, and most of those are subconscious. Planting scriptures in your spirit that light up your heart will make a huge difference in your perception of the words people say to you.

CHEER UP

Never be ashamed to rejoice in the face of contradictory circumstances. Many parents come home from work grousing over their jobs, bosses, and coworkers. They often complain about being the only Christians in their workplace. But thank God they have an opportunity to hold up light in a dark place, or that they even have a job at all in this day and age. If Christians weren't there, it would be a dark place to do business.

A bad attitude has a way of spilling over onto our children, and they consciously or unconsciously pick up on a negative attitude toward the work we do, the life we live, and the people we are supposed to love. Attitudes are caught, not taught. God releases His blessings on us when we rejoice and think on good things.

Hebrews 3:6 says, "And it is we who are [now members] of this house, if we hold fast and firm to the end our joyful and exultant confidence and sense of triumph in our hope [in Christ]." The look on our face is proof that Jesus has either won or lost the battle in our opinion. We know the Bible says He won, no matter what anyone thinks. But we need to show it by our actions, our appearance, and our attitude. They definitely speak louder than our words, and our children are watching us.

Proverbs 15:13 says a happy heart shows up on your face. The way you look is so important because you are either a billboard for the Lord or for the enemy. That is why we as Christians need to maintain a cheerful countenance. It puts everyone around you at ease when you smile. You can cause a lot of discomfort when you walk around looking depressed.

The nation of France has one of the highest rates of prescription drug use in the world since there is also a high rate of depression.[2] Some French people think it is odd when someone walks around with a smile on his face. They even go so far as to say people who are smiling all the time might be a little bit off mentally! But Christians who maintain their joy are right on spiritually. Perhaps that is why the French enjoy extreme slapstick comedy so much. They need to laugh as much as they can to stay strong!

Rejoicing was probably the last thing Job had in mind after he lost his family, his wealth, and his health. But depression would not take Job where he wanted to go. He had to change his attitude and his mouth if he wanted to see restoration in his situation. You will have to do the same thing yourself. Your tongue is like the rudder of a ship; it will move your life in different directions. It might seem awkward and strange at first, but after a time of pressing in with praise and declaring God's Word, you will see change.

After Job declared his trust in God, saying, "I know that You can do all things, and that no thought or purpose of Yours can be restrained or thwarted" (Job 42:2), the Lord blessed him exceedingly. Job had more in his latter days than he did before!

Getting cheerful in a difficult situation is vital. Do not get tense and uptight when things or people come against you—just stay in God's presence and enjoy a good laugh! You are not laughing at the problem itself. You are laughing at the fact that this problem cannot do you any permanent harm, because God is laughing with you, and He is on your side.

CHAPTER 7

Moving Toward the Light

I MOVED TO LAS Vegas in 1977 when I was in my twenties. It would be putting it mildly to say I went there reluctantly. Only the Holy Spirit, hot on my trail to bring me to salvation, could have led me to leave California's bright, golden shores for Nevada's cactus-filled desert.

Life in my hometown of Santa Barbara was like being in a veritable paradise. Actually, it was even better because I was sharing a beach house with an artist friend of mine on one of the most exclusive stretches of sand in America. My daily routine consisted of bodysurfing around 7:00 a.m. on Miramar Beach in Montecito, then going off to work at the local radio station to report the day's news. What a seemingly idyllic life at the time. But when a fellow reporter who had just moved to Nevada called and told me about a job opening at a 50,000-watt, all-news station in Las Vegas, my desire to broadcast in a larger market trumped the beach!

However, living conditions on the beach were so ideal that making a move from the ocean to the desert was a hard choice. The job opportunity got me keyed up for the moment, but that lasted only about as long as the six-hour drive east. Las Vegas in the seventies was little more than a wind-swept desert town littered with casinos lit up with bright neon signs. It was a hot place to be—but only because of the weather. After the interview, I politely declined the job offer and rushed back to the security and serenity of Santa Barbara and the ocean.

But the Nevada radio station needed a strong voice and aggressive style of reporting, so they kept calling, enticing me with better offers. When they decided to double the salary, it was the trump card. At the ripe old age of twenty-nine I left the Southern California lifestyle for a desert gambling town that had little to offer other than a good career opportunity. What I did not know at the time was that God was also waiting for me in the last place I ever thought I would ever meet Him.

Journalists from across the Western United States were being recruited to join this burgeoning enterprise. A young woman named Gail was among them. Meeting her was a defining moment for me. Much of the crew at the Santa Barbara radio station had been supportive of me, but I sensed this woman was going to be my nemesis and would try to undermine me the second I turned my back on her.

We couldn't have been more opposite. Gail had a neatly groomed appearance—beautiful long, black hair and clothes that were always immaculate and neatly pressed. I, on the other hand, was the ultimate surfer girl—fresh from the beach and a throwback to my hippie days at Berkeley in the sixties. I kept a deep tan, had long hair, and wore little or no makeup. My attire usually consisted of spaghetti-strapped sundresses.

Gail and I were at odds the moment I walked in the station door. From day one we eyed each other like pitbulls in a dogfight. We had two different points of view and were preparing to duke it out on the job for the best position.

I knew life at this Vegas station would be different, but this was a whole new ball game. After having had a seasoned veteran edit my stories at the Santa Barbara station, I was now working with neophytes. The difference in their editing experience was obvious, and it started to irritate my unregenerated mind. I thought, *Why is this person trying to change the whole tone of my writing?*

Pride rose up in me like an unruly beast. The passion to protect my work bristled in my heart. There was no way I was going to succumb to this humiliating experience. My future lay in the balance. I could lose potential job opportunities because of the stroke of one person's pen, or so I thought. A national radio syndicate from Washington DC, called for a tape of my work and invited me to audition for a position as a reporter. Even though it never panned out, I figured another opportunity might, and I wasn't about to let a newbie chop up my work like so much sushi in a California roll.

Fortunately for me and the rest of the new workforce, the Lord and poor budgeting intervened before a serious clash ensued. Everyone lost their jobs at this enterprise because it lacked both a business plan and sufficient startup capital. When the money and the advertisers ran out, the station managers departed as soon as they handed us our pink slips. We had no choice but to scour the town for other broadcasting opportunities.

FINDING COMMON GROUND

Thankfully I found another job with the local CBS Radio affiliate, but not before the Lord got hold of my life. During the interim period before I found a new position, I spotted an odd-looking geodesic dome across from my apartment. It was a church. I remembered that before I left Santa Barbara, my brother told me there were a lot of Christians in Las Vegas. Partly out of curiosity I thought, *Well, I might as well go over there on Sunday and see what is going on.*

Experiencing the worship and the preaching did not bring me to the Lord that day. But when an evangelistic team came to my door the following Tuesday and explained the plan of salvation, it was a different matter. The leader asked if I was ready to accept Jesus into my heart to be my personal Lord and Savior. However I promptly declined, not wanting to give up my partying lifestyle. But he persisted, "What if you were to die tonight?"

That made me think. Maybe it was time to turn around my life? I decided it was time to take the step and pray with him and the team. My life started to totally change right away. Old desires to drink and party immediately faded away, and my language and my life were transformed—right in the middle of the last place I would have ever thought anyone could experience salvation. It was glorious.

The Lord had a plan for my desert move,, and He caused my life to blossom like a rose.

Getting up at 3:30 a.m. to be on the air by 5:00 a.m. at this new station was grueling, but the job was a great training ground. I was hired as the news director, which allowed me to send stories all over the country to larger CBS affiliates. Although small, this station afforded lots of opportunities to hone my craft professionally, and God used my time there to train me spiritually.

My enthusiasm to expose political corruption as an investigative reporter won me favor with other reporters, and I started making Christian friends within the industry. In Las Vegas at that time, believers in the media needed to do all they could to encourage one another. So we began meeting once a month at the local Christian radio station to pray and study the Bible together. Those get-togethers were so encouraging to Christians who were being disparaged for their faith. Even then, liberal media came against reporters who were believers.

A lot of people would have been discouraged by the climate in many newsrooms at that time, but to me it was exhilarating. I saw the opposition as a sign that the Lord was with us. As Pastor John Osteen, the father of Lakewood Church pastor Joel Osteen, used to say, "If the enemy has not opposed you at least once during your day, you must not be doing anything for God!" I couldn't agree more.

Celebrities came to Las Vegas so often it seemed we were always interviewing one famous person or another. After these interviews were over, a few of us who were part of the Bible study would stay behind, witnessing to people we interviewed, such as Willie Nelson, Jane Fonda, and David Frost. Over time other Christian journalists began to join us. One day I noticed my former rival, Gail, lagging behind after one of these celebrity interviews.

After leaving the failed radio station, she had landed a job as the anchor of the city's top television station. I had seen her around, but we still were not friendly. But, as the saying goes, "If you hang around the banks long enough, you'll fall into the river." As she watched us witnessing, Gail let her curiosity about Jesus trump her dislike of my writing style and laid-back Southern California ways.

Gail was born again not long after that day she stayed behind to hear us talk about our faith. Slowly the love of God and our joy in Jesus finally bonded us together. Instead of looking at each other from the opposite side of the fence and living as archenemies, Gail and I found ourselves working together to reach people for the Lord. Whenever the opportunity presented itself, she joined us in witnessing to celebrities we interviewed.

Later I was promoted to the larger ABC-affiliated station. Although Las Vegas was a country-western bastion, the station personnel, especially the manager, were vehemently opposed to anything related to Jesus. Nevertheless, the love of God continued to flow out of me, and I witnessed whenever the Lord gave me an opportunity.

Next on God's list was the disc jockey, Vince, whose desk faced mine through the glass station booth. I constantly looked for opportunities to talk with him about the Lord, and God gave me several. After a month or so, Vince also accepted Christ and started going to the same little church many of us media Christians had been attending in north Las Vegas.

At church one Sunday, Vince met Gail and they eventually started dating, then got married. The love of God changed everything. Instead of being at odds with a fellow reporter, I ended up being a bridesmaid at Gail's wedding!

God turned this awkward and potentially strife-filled situation around for good. He can do the same thing with your friends and family if you trust Him and follow His leading. He is an expert at making broken relationships whole, but He does require that you stay in communication with Him.

BROKEN BUT NOT HOPELESS

The enemy loves it when we think a relationship is broken beyond repair. He loves to see us fighting one another and giving no thought to the possibility of finding common ground. But as Christians, we need to quit fighting with people, especially our family and coworkers, and love and respect them instead. We need to show them we respect them enough to hear what they have to say, even when we do not agree with them. That we value their views, pray for them, and are an example of Jesus' love.

This is exactly where praise becomes vital. Even in the most exhausting conflict, if you enter into God's presence, you can rise above the situation and start to experience the victory in your heart before you ever see anything in the natural. Your energy and strength will come back to you.

Fight on in faith, not with people—for we wrestle not with flesh and blood but with principalities and powers (Ephesians 6:12). Press in to God when a relationship is strained, and you'll find peace and joy in His presence. When you see nothing but sorrow and disappointment around you, make a choice to speak life into that situation. What you say will make all the difference in the outcome you receive.

You have to stand firm and still move in the love of God. Legalism will invite judgment and strife into the situation and leave you paralyzed in unforgiveness. Religion is stiff and ritualistic, but a relationship with God flows with adventure, excitement, and love for all people. Spending time in His presence is where you will get the victory when the missiles start falling and you feel like you have lost your defense system. The Lord is the final judge. He has called us to love others as Christ loved us. As you praise the Lord in a difficult relationships, Joy is the oil that lubricates your heart again. It will flow you into peace where you will find victory.

CHAPTER 8

Shout It Out

IF YOU'VE EVER attended a sports event, you know die-hard fans don't sit passively and quietly watch the game. Whether it's football, baseball, basketball, or soccer, fans will scream at the top of their lungs to cheer on their favorite team. They will jump to their feet. Green Bay Packers fans in Wisconsin go so far as to wear plastic "cheesehead" hats to express their home team loyalty. This dairy-producing state clearly is not ashamed.

Most of the time Christians too are on their feet, cheering for their favorite team during ball games. We express ourselves exuberantly when we see a hero, a sports giant, someone who has pushed the envelope and won despite all odds. We are inspired by their ability or sheer tenacity to get the ball where it needs to go.

If we can cheer for a person whose strength is in throwing, shooting, catching, or hitting a ball, why would we suddenly dampen our enthusiasm when we approach God? He is the ultimate hero, the One who paid the price for our salvation. He has declared victory over every obstacle we will ever face. He has already defeated the enemy, no matter how things may seem. Isn't that something worth shouting about?

When you rejoice in the face of what the devil is trying to do in your life, you get a release. You let go of the stress of trying to find an answer to your problem on your own, knowing that God has already taken care of it. Your shouts of praise attest to the impending victory and the devil's ultimate defeat.

Psalm 47:1 tells us, "O clap your hands, all you peoples! Shout to God with the voice of triumph and songs of joy." We honor God when we exuberantly express our joy to Him. Being silent and looking downcast do not equal reverence. God wants to hear our praises.

You can't justify your silence by saying, "God knows how I feel about Him. I don't have to be loud." That is like saying, "God knows I am sorry for what I have done. I don't have to ask Him for forgiveness." The Lord doesn't work by mental assent. It's not enough for you to simply believe Him in your head. God wants to hear your voice at full pitch, praising and honoring Him.

There is no forgiveness without repentance (Luke 3:3). All Bible believing churches agree that we have to repent in order to be saved, but not all of them teach that we should express ourselves exuberantly in praise and worship. Some say that quiet worship is the only proper way to honor God. But God gave us our emotions for more reasons than to yelling at sports events. He wants us to use our emotions to display our love and gratitude toward Him, to pour out our hearts in thankfulness to a wonderful Creator.

The boring and stiff traditions of men will make the Word of God of none effect in our lives, and they certainly make it unpalatable to a younger generation. Just because you have always done something one way does not make it the right way. The tradition of men makes the word of God of none effect. (See Mark 7:13.)

I once heard a story about a mother who was teaching her daughter how to cook a ham. "First you cut off each end of the ham and put it in the roasting pan," the mother said. "Set it in the oven and then check it later to see if you need to cover it so the top doesn't burn."

The daughter asked, "Why do you cut off the ends of the ham?"

The mother replied, "I don't know. That's the way I was taught to do it."

So the mother and daughter called Grandma and asked her why she cut off the ends of the ham. She said, "That's how my mother taught me to do it."

They then called Great-Grandma and asked her why the ends were cut off the ham. She said, "Well, the only roasting pan I had was too small for the ham, so I always cut off the ends to make it fit." These women had been following a handed-down tradition and as a result, had been throwing away perfectly good pieces of meat!

How often do we miss out on good things God has for us because we're following a lifeless method of doing something? Listen, if you want to experience something new in your life, if you want better results than you've had in the past, you have to leave the old wineskins behind. Luke 5:37–39 says, "And no one pours new wine into old wineskins; if he does, the fresh wine will burst the skins and it will be spilled and the skins will be ruined (destroyed). But new wine must be put in fresh wineskins. And no one after drinking old wine immediately desires new wine, for he says, The old is good or better."

Legalistic religion and the gospel do not mix; one will ruin the other. No one who is satisfied with dead religion will want to taste the new unless he has a change of heart. That is why we have to allow the Holy Spirit to make us new creatures in Christ.

The wineskins referred to in Luke 5 were made out of animal hides. Over time, the skins would become inflexible and set in shape. If new wine were poured into the old wineskins, the gas of fermentation would cause the wineskins to stretch and burst. Religion will make your heart inflexible, but relationship with God gives you the desire to remain pliable before Him. When God is prompting you to abandon unfruitful methods and do it His way, have a hearing ear be willing and obedient. God's plans for you and your family are good. He wants you to move into a fresh and new life, one that is free and filled with joy and rejoicing.

REST IN GOD, NOT RELIGION

When you start looking at your family struggles from God's point of view, you can start to rest. Hebrews 4:3 says, "For we which have believed do enter into rest" (KJV). Resting in the Spirit means being free from whatever worries or disturbs you. Some people cannot rest mentally and emotionally because they are so easily upset. Every little nuisance distracts them, and they always feel hassled.

Rest does not mean freedom from all worry; it means freedom from being so easily bothered by whatever disturbs your rest. *Rest* means to be inwardly quiet, composed, and peaceful.[1] To enter into God's rest means to be at peace with God by accepting His gift of salvation (Romans 5:1) and to live in the perfect peace He gives (Isaiah 26:3). It means to be free from guilt, both real and false. Rest means to know your sin is forgiven.

God's rest is the end of legalistic works and the experience of peace in the total forgiveness of God. *Rest* can mean to lie down, be settled, fixed, and secure.[2] There is no more running in circles. In God's rest, we are forever established in Christ. We are freed from being tossed about by every wind of doctrine, every idea or fad that blows our way. In Christ, we are rooted, grounded, and immoveable. That is the rest of a joyful Christian.

Rest involves remaining stable. In other words, to rest in something means to maintain confidence in it. To enter God's rest, therefore, means to enjoy the perfect, unshakable confidence of salvation in our Lord. We have no more reason to fear. We have absolute trust and confidence in God's power to deliver us.

Resting in prayer can and will change things. Jesus never leaves you or forsakes you, and He hears you the first time you pray. It is up to you to stand in confidence that God has already answered, knowing it is His will that your house be saved, even when you cannot see the manifestation of that answer.

When God's response is delayed, there is a reason. He may be using the situation to help you mature. It may be time to "examine your ways" and ask God if there is something He wants to see change in or about you. You may think bringing your children back to the Lord is all about their spiritual needs, but actually the lack of love in your Christian walk may be exactly what is keeping them from rededicating their lives to Christ. Of course, their rebellion is part of a demonic attack on the plans God has for them, but you have to rise up against it and not let it roll you out flat like a piece of biscuit dough.

It's funny how much attention people who claim not to believe in God pay to Christians. They notice when we display our Christian bumper stickers and zoom down the road not wearing our seat belts and texting all at the same time! People who are outside the church are looking for truth, to see if we really practice what we preach. It makes a huge impact on them and the kingdom when we actually live our faith out loud.

The ministry of the Los Angeles Dream Center saw a 70 percent crime reduction in the six blocks surrounding their facility when volunteers started reaching out to serve their neighbors with no agenda except to show them the love of Jesus with their actions.[3] They painted fences, cleaned up yards, supplied food, and donated furniture, and these simple acts changed hardened hearts into open minds. Today this huge ministry, which is housed in a former hospital, reaches some forty thousand people each month.[4] Those people may never have listened to a preacher, but they experienced the love of Christ because they saw the gospel in action. As 1 Corinthians 13:13 says, love is the greatest spiritual gift of all.

We cannot afford to be inflexible on this point. We have to

be open to growth, which always involves change. Change can be frightening. Jesus was a revolutionary in His time. To even consider defying Jewish tradition and the rabbinical ways was total heresy, but the gospel Jesus taught brought life to a culture steeped in legalistic bondage and for thousands of years, people have been longing for the love and freedom He has to offer.

Knowledge and revelation of the new things God wants to do come gradually; He gives us only enough we can handle at one time, lest we choke on it. Yet even more important than knowledge is wisdom. We can have all the knowledge we want, but without wisdom, we won't know how to apply the knowledge God gives.

HE IS ALIVE IN YOUR PRAISE

I always told my children there is no neutral in God; we are either going forward or going backward. Praising, worshiping, and rejoicing propel us forward in our walk with God. Let yourself rejoice over God's goodness, if for no other reason than because He has kept you alive and has given you such a great salvation. And be expressive in praise!

Psalm 22:3 says the Lord actually *inhabits* the praises of His people. God's presence *lives* in our praises. That is such a powerful thought. When you really meditate on the meaning of that verse, you will be praising and rejoicing throughout your day. When I am in a perplexing place, I often go into my ofice or prayer closet, close the door, raise my hands, and ask God to help me deal with the situation, show me what to do, or even forgive me. His answers

Joyful Parent

always come when I submit the situation to Him. God knows of your trouble before it happens. He also has your victory if you let Him fight your battle.

It would be frustrating for a coach to have the game plan all laid out for the team during the championship series but see the team lose because they decided to follow their own plays instead of listening to the leader. God's way is not against you; He is for you. He has the answer before you realize there is a problem. He is waiting to see you dance your way through the problem, praising Him from mountaintop to mountaintop. You are not denying the valleys are there; you are just denying their right to dominate you.

It is the same process with your own walk with God. You get what you expect. When you thank God before the victory appears, your expectant attitude leads you into victory. Your joy helps you stay strong in Him while the strongholds around you come tumbling down.

The Lord wants to hear you pray, praise, and thank Him before you see any evidence of the answer. John 16:24 says, "Ask, and you will receive, that your joy may be full" (NKJV). He wants you full of joy as an outward sign of His goodness in your life. He wants the world to see how good it is to live life His way.

REFUSE TO KEEP SILENT

As technology becomes a bigger part of life, it seems like you need a password for everything. Each time you use your computer or cell phone and, perhaps, even to enter your apartment and your car, you have to put in that code. You cannot gain access without the correct combination of letters or numbers. Your password is the key.

But the most effective code for you to access daily is the password of praise: "Blessed are the people who know the passwords of praise, who shout on parade in the bright presence of GOD. Delighted, they dance all day long; they know who you are, what you do—they can't keep it quiet!" (Psalm 89:15–16, THE MESSAGE). The password of praise opens God's heart and releases the answers you so desperately need to turn the situation around.

As the last part of verse 16 says, "They can't keep it quiet!" When you dance before the Lord, you are making a loud prayer request. You are shouting in the middle of a parade. Think of the annual Macy's Thanksgiving Day Parade or the Rose Parade in Pasadena, California, on New Year's Day. People are shouting and cheering as the magnificent floats pass by them. They are not hiding away in sorrow and shame.

The church we pastored in Southern Caifornia in the eighties used to sponsor floats in a local parade every summer. We decorated those floats from top to bottom with brilliant types of flowers. The women from the congregation would wear colorful red skirts and flowers in their hair, while the men would don red sashes and Spanish hats. Church members would sing and dance all the way down the main streets, praising the Lord in front of everyone. We did not hold anything back because we knew God loved the display; He was being magnified by praise in front of the whole town.

When I am rejoicing before the Lord, I am expressing myself in the presence of the King! And He is so worthy of it. He deserves my highest praise.

So jump into the parade! Thank God He always causes you to triumph in Christ. Honor Him by showing Him off to the world with a happy heart, joyful countenance, and a mouth full of praise. When we make Him bigger than the circumstances around us, the situation will start to change right before our eyes. The enemy will attempt to intimidate us, but we have nothing to fear. Jesus took care of fear at the cross—and gave us a spirit of power, love, and a sound mind instead.

Jesus was not concerned about going to the cross publicly, and neither should we care about praising Him openly and displaying an attitude of joy and exuberant thankfulness for it. His triumph at the cross still lives on, redeeming people from hell and the grave more than two thousand years later. That is eternal longevity.

Colossians 2:15 says, "[God] disarmed the principalities and powers that were ranged against us and made a bold display and public example of them, in triumphing over them in Him and in it [the cross]." He didn't just defeat the odd demon that comes against us occasionally; Jesus whipped every single devil that ever has, or ever will, come against us. The problem is, we have to stop staring at what the enemy is doing and acknowledge thankfully what God has already done.

If Christians would fight principalities and powers and not one another, we would win every single time. Our fight is not with human beings but the enemy. Remember the prophet Daniel? The angel told him his prayer was heard from the very first day he prayed it, but demonic forces fought to prevent the prayer from being answered (Daniel 10).

The same is true of us. Our prayers for our children are heard the first day we pray them, but Satan will try to block the answer. He will send any obstacle he can to get our children off course and away from God's will. If we magnify the work of the enemy over Jesus's resurrection power, we will end up right where the devil wants us—in a prison of fear and worry because we have believed the lie that God's Word is not true.

The devil is the master of deception. Remember what the serpent said in the Garden of Eden: "Hath God *really* said?" Yes, devil, God really *did* say that our children shall return from the land of the enemy, that they were trained up in the way they should go and when they are old they will not depart from it. And His Word is the same yesterday, today, and forever.

The flower fades, but God's Word never passes away. Meditating on and decreeing Scripture is a powerful weapon against the enemy. We have to take control of our thoughts, and that begins with our mouths. This is a major offensive tactic we have in resisting the enemy.

Rejoice before God. Thank the Lord that He already won the battle the devil is trying to convince us is lost. Celebrate Jesus! He is Lord over our families. Our fight is not with our sons or daughters. When we chastise and argue with them out of a heart filled with anger and unforgiveness, we will only drive them further away from God. It was the love of God that drew us to repentance, and that is what brings our children back as well. God comes to us with an open hand of mercy and grace, not a finger of judgment and condemnation.

CHAPTER 9

The Power of the Anointing

JESUS WAS WALKING down the road in a crowd of hundreds of people when He suddenly stopped because He felt something. He turned around to His disciples and asked, "Who touched My clothes?" This wasn't an ordinary crowd; there were literally people everywhere. But when a woman who had been bleeding for twelve years touched the hem of His garment, believing she would be made whole, Jesus felt something leave Him. Mark 5:30 says Jesus immediately knew "virtue" had gone out of Him (KJV). The woman with the issue of blood tapped into Jesus, the Source of healing.

The anointing of God is not a theoretical concept; it is a substance. It is the presence of God's person that rested upon Jesus. Put even more simply, the anointing is the power of the Holy Spirit. That power will draw your children back to God and heal your relationship with them. That power is what enables you to walk through the most difficult times with your kids. That power is what will wake you up at 2:00 a.m. to pray for your teen when he is still not home. His presence is the power that will protect that same youth when shots ring out at the party he snuck off to, and that power is the only explanation you will have for why he was able to get out of there untouched, despite the bullet sprays throughout the room from a gang firing across the street.

If you want to see your children restored to God and your relationship repaired, you must learn to cooperate with the Holy Spirit. You cannot do it without Him.

In Mark 5, it was the faith of the woman with the issue of blood that broke into Jesus's power. She touched Him by faith, believing she would be healed if she did. And her faith made her whole (v. 34). This story again proves that personal faith will move God to provide what we have been praying and believing for.

YOU ARE NEVER FORGOTTEN

When the woman touched Jesus, He was on His way to the home of Jairus, a ruler of the synagogue. Jairus' daughter was near death, and he asked Jesus to come to his house and heal her. Jesus was on His way there when He felt virtue leave Him and stopped to ask, "Who touched me?"

When Jesus stopped to look for one person who touched Him in a crowd of people, Jairus was probably wondering if Jesus still remembered his petition. He had been worshiping at Jesus' feet long before this woman had come on the scene. His petition reached Jesus long before the woman even got near Jesus' garment. But now Jesus had stopped everything to heal this woman. Had He forgotten about Jairus?

How often do we feel that way? How often do we think Jesus has forgotten about us?

While Jesus was still speaking with the woman with the issue of blood, a man from Jairus' house came up and told him not to trouble Jesus any longer because his daughter was dead (Luke 8:49). Talk about hope being destroyed! But Jesus heard the man, and He told Jairus, "Do not be seized with alarm or struck with fear; simply believe [in Me as able to do this], and she shall be made well" (v. 50). And she was. Jesus went to Jairus' house, told the girl to wake up, and immediately she was well.

If you think God has forgotten your prayer, wonder no longer. He remembers and keeps every prayer you have ever prayed. They are kept as tears in His bottle. Psalm 56:8 says, "You number and record my wanderings; put my tears into Your bottle—are they not in Your book?"

The Lord takes account of all the times you have cried out to Him concerning your children. Don't give up now. Keep on believing. We'll never know how many times a prayer failed to get an answer because the person stopped believing. That answer may have been around the corner but never materialized because the person gave up on it

When Jairus heard that his daughter was no longer sick but dead, he could have easily lost it. In fact, he may have thought the situation was hopeless in the few moments between Luke 8:49, when he heard the bad news, and Luke 8:50, when Jesus told him not to be alarmed. Jairus chose to keep believing, and Jesus did more than he ever imagined. Jesus did more than pull Jairus's daughter back from the brink of death—He pulled her back from death itself. He did something the people at Jairus's house didn't think was possible and as a result, Jesus raised everyone's faith.

Never give up! God will not fail you. Don't stop believing He will answer your prayer. No matter what His reasons for delaying His answer, God never forgets us. He is faithful to do what He said He would.

If you aren't seeing an answer to your prayer, God may want to teach you to trust Him even when it seems all hope is gone. He may want to work out something in your life, something that may be keeping your child from returning to Him. Or maybe there are people around you who need to witness the miracle to raise their faith.

A Resting Place

After the great flood in Genesis 8, Noah released a dove from the ark to see if the waters had receded and if there was dry ground. But the dove found no resting place and returned to the ark. So Noah waited another seven days then released the dove again. This time the bird returned with an olive branch in her mouth. When he sent her out across the waters a third time, the dove didn't return at all.

The Holy Spirit is always looking for a resting place in our hearts, but some people may not be ready for Him yet. When you are in darkness, even a little light hurts your eyes. But the good news is He never stops looking for an opportunity to land.

We might think it strange that the Holy Spirit hindered Paul from going into Asia Minor in Acts 16. After all, he was on his way to preach the gospel; why would the Holy Spirit want to prevent that? Because the Macedonians were not ready for Him yet! They would have stoned Paul to pieces. So he waited on the Lord for a year and then went back there unhindered. Paul ended up starting a school of ministry that lasted for three years!

RELEASE GOD'S PRESENCE

The gospel is not just a ministry of words; it is the good news releasing God's presence into the earth, like the aroma of a rare perfume permeating the atmosphere. Jesus is the Word of God made flesh, and every time He spoke, those words became spirit. Why is that important? Paul says in Romans 14:17, "The kingdom of God is not meat and drink; but righteousness, and peace, and joy in the Holy Ghost" (KJV). In other words, the kingdom of God is *in* the Holy Spirit.

When we say what the Father is saying, we literally impart His presence into our environment through our speech. It changes the atmosphere. If we have tapped into the heart of the Father and something is released through our mouth that reflects God, then the hearer is presented with options he never considered before.

Jesus is telling you today that your answer is within reach. It is at hand. But what are your affections anchored to? That is what is going to be released from you, just as the healing power of God was released from Peter's shadow as he walked down the road in Acts 5. What do you live conscious of? If you are aware of depression in your heart, your shadow is not going to affect anyone. People who are depressed are turned inward; they are thinking of themselves. And when we are turned inward, although our spirit has the capacity to release the presence of God, we have in fact become a Dead Sea. The Dead Sea is a place where water flows in but nothing goes out and for that reason, everything in that sea is stagnant and lifeless.

This happens to us as believers when we get wrapped up in fear and anxiety and become focused on our problems, when we become self-absorbed and don't apply His solutions to our issues. You may think criticizing yourself and over analyzing yourself makes you humble, but actually it causes you to be preoccupied with who you are not instead of with who He is. False humility will never take you to your destiny. Only true humility will. The joy Jesus had was not there just to change His circumstances; it was upon Him to alter the atmosphere around Him.

When you are worried about being fearful and anxious about the future of your children, you have restricted the flow of the anointing to you. Why does this happen? Because the Spirit of God flows through your love and compassion, and fear will stop that flow. You are drawn to an individual with a heart of mercy because that person has allowed the Holy Spirit to release His blessing through him or her.

Jesus's impact was so significant in three and a half years that what He accomplished could not be contained in one book. That is because He allowed the Holy Spirit to rest on Him unrestrained that whole time. There is a presence that rests upon you, according to God's purposes for you on this earth. If ever the world needed to see the power of God manifest in the earth, it is now. Don't let fear and pride dam up God's provision and power. Let Him release His power through you unfettered so He can use you to change the atmosphere in your home.

DON'T LOSE HOPE

There is a powerful passage in Isaiah 61 that seems to have been written for anyone who trusts God but is going through something.. It says, "The Spirit of the Lord GOD is upon me; because the LORD hath anointed me to preach good tidings unto the meek . . . to give unto them beauty for ashes, the oil of joy for mourning, the garment of praise for the spirit of heaviness; that they might be called trees of righteousness, the planting of the LORD, that he might be glorified" (vv. 1–3, KJV).

In verse 3, the prophet is basically saying, "Thank You, Lord, that I am finished with mourning and a life of ashes." You have to "future think." The enemy tries to hand us a load of defeat when our children go off into a different path. He whispers in our ears, "All the work you did for your children, all the prayers you prayed for them didn't work!" But we have to consider the source. The devil is a liar and the father of lies (John 8:44). We have to see his condemnation for what it is. We must realize that Satan is lying to us once again, and we have to kick that thought out of our heads and start thanking God that our children shall "return from the enemy's land," as Jeremiah 31:16 promises. We have to make up our minds once and for all that God's Word works when we work it.

Isaiah 61:3 goes on to say, "For the beauty of Your Spirit is upon me with *great joy* in my heart. My life is full of praise instead of heaviness. You have planted me like a strong, graceful oak for Your glory" (author paraphrase). He plants us in strength when we can praise, when we rejoice despite what we see—because what we see with our natural eyes is not what He sees with His supernatural eyes.

A ministry friend had a daughter who had been in a terrible car accident. The girl was almost killed and ended up in a coma for several weeks. Her physical condition was deteriorating with each passing day. The doctors and nurses would enter the hospital room, examine her motionless body and shake their heads in despair. They constantly advised the mother that it might be time to pull the plug on her daughter, who was only in her early thirties. However, this mother was a fighter and was not willing to lose her only daughter to the enemy. She knew hope could be encouraged through what people could see of this girl.

She found a picture of her daughter at a horse show wearing her full riding habit and jumping over a gate on a beautifully groomed horse. This mother had the picture enlarged to poster size and put it over the girl's hospital bed. Every time the doctors and nurses entered the room, that picture stared them in the face and reminded them of what the girl was supposed to look like. It became a portrait of hope for the future.

These professionals started to get a glimpse what God saw for this girl—a body that was whole, well, and strong. As their line of sight changed every time they walked into that room, the girl started to change, and eventually she came out of the coma. She walked out of that hospital, strong and courageous, because people started to visualize a young woman that was healed and whole.

We see things one way in the natural, but God's perspective is supernatural. He sees the end from the beginning, but we see only in part.

Here's a piece of wisdom: The next time the enemy tries to hand you a bill of goods about your family, think of King David and the way he danced before the ark of the covenant. Do a dance right in front of the enemy's eyes, and let him see that his defeat is imminent. Your praise is preparing the way for the King to enter in. Your rejoicing is actually building the road for your breakthrough to manifest!

Joyful Parent

CHAPTER 10

Start Talking Right

EXCEEDING JOY? I'M thinking, Are you kidding me? Lord, I can't even laugh out loud in the middle of this situation, and You're asking me to rejoice exceedingly? The Lord must have wanted to shock me out of despair. The situation in my family was not good and seemed to be getting worse when the Holy Spirit took me to Psalm 43:2: "For You are the God of my strength [my Stronghold—in Whom I take refuge]." I began to speak the Word, even though I didn't see any signs of change. And slowly I began to see God bring healing in the situation.

Sometimes we just need to speak to ourselves and remind ourselves *who* we are in Christ, *what* our rights and privileges are as God's children, and *why* we have the authority we do. We have to start declaring that what we have already prayed for is so and delight in the Lord as we wait for the victory to manifest.

If you are believing God to bring your child back to Him, declare it on a daily basis. Ask the Holy Spirit to drop specific scriptures into your heart that speak to you about His purpose and plan for your child. He will do it, and you will start to see results.

Don't be ashamed to recruit faithful prayer partners to

agree with you. (Just make sure they are people who are sincere intercessors and not gossipers who repeat all your prayer requests!) Then pray aloud the scriptures God gives you, inserting your loved one's name into the verse. God watches over *His* Word to perform it, not yours (Jeremiah 1:12). That is why it is so important to pray His Word over your own words.

God spoke the world into existence, and His Word has the same creative power today as it did then. Isaiah 55:11 says, "So shall My word be that goes forth out of My mouth: it shall not return to Me void [without producing any effect, useless], but it shall accomplish that which I please and purpose, and it shall prosper in the thing for which I sent it."

God's Word has a built-in, self-fulfilling power. Because God's Word is truth (John 17:17), it is required to do what it says it will do. When the Holy Spirit reveals to you the power of praying God's Word, you will gain a fresh perspective in your prayer life and see that the creative power in your mouth is a freedom creator and answer maker.

Of course, everyone has a free will, but God wants you to call your children out into the light. There is great spiritual power in calling people into the Lord. First Peter 2:9 says God called us "out of darkness into His marvelous light." Loved ones who have been away from God have been making decisions in the dark. But when you start calling them out of darkness into the light of God, they can change their minds based on the light they are entering into. When you pray, "Father, I call [insert name] out of the darkness into Your marvelous light," you are giving that person an opportunity to come into the light and make decisions for their future based on light and not darkness.

As we have discussed throughout this book, God gives us authority as believers. But remember, you are praying to the Lord, not to people. The people around you, including your child or unsaved relative, are not the ones who need to hear your prayers. Only God needs to hear them. God watches over His Word to perform it. He is the One who is going to bring the answer to pass.

He wants us standing firm on that truth. Instead of begging God when you are interceding for your children, start speaking the Word. One woman who started doing this saw four of her family members come back to the Lord in eight months. She had been praying and witnessing to them for years with no positive response. But after she started praying the Word with their names inserted into scriptures God gave her, those family members started asking her how to get to church.

This same woman prayed for her unsaved father, who lived in another state. He would have nothing to do with the Lord. So she simply spoke the Word of God over her dad and believed the Lord would watch over His Word to perform it, as Jeremiah 1:12 promises. In a short amount of time her father, who was a widower, met a woman he was interested in dating. She was saved and attended church, so he had to go with her to church to get to know her. After going to church for a while, he got saved and totally committed his life to the Lord.

All this man's daughter did was pray the Word with her dad's name inserted into scriptures the Holy Spirit had given her. She had nothing in the natural to do with her father finding Jesus. She never took him to church or shoved God down his throat. All she did was sit back and watch God fulfill His Word. She rested in the fact that God is well able.

As we begin to speak God's Word over our families, we have to put aside feelings of unforgiveness. Whether your loved ones get to heaven is a far more important issue than whatever differences you may have on earth. When you sow seeds of love and acceptance, those seeds produce a harvest. You are not the Holy Ghost, Jr. You just do your part and allow the Holy Spirit to do the rest. He may use you to lead your loved one to salvation or to rededicate his life to the Lord, or He may use someone else. What is important is that He *will* accomplish His Word.

STAND IN FAITH

As I mentioned before, it is important that you not continually mull over and talk about what is going on in your child's life at the moment. Your child may be dealing with drugs, alcohol, and other addictions, but those strongholds have to come down as the truth of God's Word is consistently declared. If you are always talking about how much trouble your loved one is in, the situation will not change. He will remain in the bound state you are always saying he is in. As the saying goes, insanity is doing the same thing over and over again and expecting different results!

Talk about your children as if they are already walking in the full light of the Lord. Act as though they are saved. Treat them with respect; don't talk down to them. They know they are missing the mark, but they need to find the way out, and they must be convinced themselves that Jesus is that way.

Honor the good things your children do, even if it is something as simple as getting to class on time. You open the door to your children's hearts when you show them respect. You demonstrate to them that you actually believe they can change for the better. Your opinion matters so much to them, although they will usually never let you know that face-to-face.

There was couple in ministry whose daughter was born again and filled with the Holy Ghost at four years of age. Raised in church, she was at every prayer meeting and was even her mom's prayer partner as she got older. But during the girl's senior year in high school, she started to become a little withdrawn and developed a strange attitude. Her friends started to influence her away from the Lord. Her mom decided it was time to begin some serious prayer. When this woman and her husband got up in the morning and started making the bed, they would agree in prayer for their daughter. They would ask Him to open the eyes of her understanding and give her wisdom to make godly choices.

A couple of months later the mother was sitting in the den of her house, and as her daughter walked past, she suddenly stopped in the doorway, stomped her foot, and said, "Stop praying for me. You are ruining my life." Then she walked away.

This woman immediately went to her husband and told him what their daughter did. She said, "Let's continue praying for her and help ruin her life." (This woman has a serious sense of humor!) The couple continued to stand in the gap. A few more months went by, and it was time for the daughter to register for college. She came to her mother and asked if they could pray together about which school she should attend. So they went to the girl's room and prayed that God would give her wisdom. After they finished praying, the daughter asked her mom what she should do.

The mother told her daughter, "It doesn't matter what I think. What is God telling you?" Her daughter said, "I am supposed to go to Bible school." Her mom said she knew their prayers for their daughter were changing things, but the way God answered them still amazes her to this day. He turned the situation completely around. Her daughter attended Bible school for three years and finished up in worship school. She is now a lead worshiper in an Oklahoma church.

When Jesus called Simon Peter into the ministry in Matthew 16:18–19, He called him *Petros*, which in the Greek signifies a large piece of rock. Just two chapters earlier that word would not have described Peter. He started to walk on water with Jesus but became so frightened by the winds and waves that he almost drowned (Matthew 14:28–32). Peter talked a good talk, but like many of us, he was not ready to walk the walk. When the going got rough, Peter allowed fear to almost make him sink. But at the last moment Peter cried out to the Lord, and "instantly Jesus reached out His hand and caught and held him, saying to him, O you of little faith, why do you doubt?" (v. 31).

Two chapters later, in Matthew 16:15, Peter learned from his mistake. When Jesus asked the disciples who they believed He was, Peter answered, "You are the Christ, the Son of the living God" (v. 16). Peter declared that Jesus was the anointed Messiah. He had come a long way in his faith, and Jesus recognized it, which is why He called him a rock. Jesus saw that Peter was growing in his ability to believe Jesus was the Savior of the world. He was not all the way there, of course, but at least he was making progress, like all of us.

When Jesus called Peter a rock, He was letting Peter know that by acknowledging Jesus's lordship, he was displaying the kind of unshakable faith Jesus would build His church on, "and the gates of hell shall not prevail against it" (v. 18, KJV). As long as you consistently walk in faith and acknowledge that Jesus is Lord over your children, the powers of hell cannot prevail against you either.

SHOOT AND KEEP ON SHOOTING

Praise and rejoicing are the highest form of warfare in the spiritual battle in which we are involved. An old Scottish proverb says, "If there's no blood on your kilt, you are just a dancer." If you had or are having family problems, keep thanking God. This doesn't mean there won't be confrontation, but you will be aware that the Lord is fighting your battles for you.

You can remove many obstacles that would keep your child from repenting by asking him to forgive you for any way you may have failed him. Have you hurt your children by not being there for them or allowing your anger to get out of control? Tell them you are sorry for the way you acted. Determine to stay calm in the midst of turmoil. Let peace umpire the situation, not your emotions.

As much as you may want to intervene in a situation, you cannot always protect your child from facing the consequences of his decisions. If you ask Him, God will give you the wisdom to distinguish the fine line between having a tender heart toward your children and allowing them to face the music. God may use the consequence to bring the prodigal to repentance.

Even if you don't see immediate results, stay strong and do not let the enemy discourage you. Being discouraged is really just that—to be *dis*-couraged, or to be without courage. The Lord is always telling us to *take* courage; we must possess it and hold it tightly in our hearts.

In 2 Kings 13:15–19, King Jehoash faced a major enemy in the army of Syria. The frightened king ran to Elisha and begged him for wisdom.

> *And Elisha said to him, Take bow and arrows. And he took bow and arrows. And he said to the king of Israel, Put your hand upon the bow. And he put his hand upon it, and Elisha put his hands upon the king's hands. And he said, Open the window to the east. And he opened it. Then Elisha said, Shoot. And he shot. And he said, The Lord's arrow of victory, the arrow of victory over Syria. For you shall smite the Syrians in Aphek till you have destroyed them.*
>
> *Then he said, Take the arrows. And he took them. And he said to the king of Israel, Strike on the ground. And he struck three times and stopped. And the man of God was angry with him and said, You should have struck five or six times; then you would have struck down Syria until you*

had destroyed it. But now you shall strike Syria down only three times.

When King Jehoash came to Elisha, the prophet told him to take a bow and arrows. In those days, these were weapons of war. So Elisha was telling Jehoash to get ready to fight his enemy. He even assured the king that God would be with him in the battle, just as He is with us. But God wants us, unlike Jehoash, to be persistent. He wants us to shoot our arrows and not give up if results are not immediate.

In verse 17, Elisha declared that the arrow the king put in his bow was "the arrow of the LORD's deliverance, and the arrow of deliverance from Syria: for thou shall smite the Syrians in Aphek, till thou have consumed them" (KJV). Acts such as these were the ancient method of declaring war. A herald would cry with a loud voice, "I wage war against you!" He would then give his reasons for war and shoot an arrow or throw a spear into the country to be invaded. This was considered enough warning of a warlike intention, and hostilities would begin thirty days later if no peace could be struck in the meantime.

After essentially telling Jehoash to declare war on Syria, Elisha instructed the king to take the arrows and strike the ground. King Jehoash struck the ground three times and stopped. Instead of being satisfied that Jehoash followed his instructions, the prophet got mad. After all that preparation with the bow, King Jehoash didn't get it that persistence is the key to victory. Three strikes were not going to get the job done. Had the King struck the ground five or six times, he would have annihilated the Syrians instead of just putting a dent in their ranks.

The king lost a total victory because he gave up too easily. We have to do the opposite. We must declare war on the enemy and be persistent enough to defeat him entirely. We cannot just make a dent in the battle for our children. We have to see it through to victory.

God Never Fails Us

Second Corinthians 1:20 says, "For all the promises of God in him [Jesus] are yea, and in him Amen, unto the glory of God by us" (KJV). And we are told in 1 Kings 8:56, "There hath not failed one word of all his good promises, which he promised by the hand of Moses his servant" (KJV).

God is clearly telling us in these passages that He never fails us, but it doesn't always seem that way. If God never fails, why haven't we seen our children come back to Him yet? If all the promises in God's Word belong to us, why don't we have them? Because we live in a fallen world, and the enemy will do everything in his power to rob us of the healing, deliverance, freedom, and victory Christ's death secured for us. Satan is the god of this world, but as children of God we have authority over all of his power (Luke 10:19). It's our responsibility to exercise that authority by agreeing with God's Word and rejecting the lies of the enemy.

If a police officer catches someone speeding, he has all the justification in the world to write that driver a ticket. But if the officer does not chase that driver down, he has chosen not to exercise the authority that is rightfully his. You can read this whole book and glean some great revelation out of it for household salvation and changing your attitude toward your children. But if you don't use what you have been given, you might as well throw it in the trash. Your gifts will increase when you use them and decrease if you do not.

Jesus said, "These things have I spoken unto you ... that your joy might be full" (John 15:11, KJV). We have to stay passionate about praying for our children. It is not the size of the dog in the fight; it is the size of the fight in the dog. We don't measure horsepower by the exhaust; we measure horsepower by its ability to carry the load.

Take that joy back from the devil's clutches that he has stolen from you. You don't have to wait for tomorrow when everything is perfect. You can get happy right now! The Holy Ghost has joy. He can lay you out on the floor and make you laugh and be full of His joy no matter *what* is going on around you.

Joyful Parent

CHAPTER 11

Shake It Off

YOUR PROBLEMS IN life can be your greatest opportunities. It took me a while to see it, but God had a plan for the parenting challenges I faced. He would use the situation to bring glory to Himself and to encourage other parents going through similar situations. In Acts 28, the apostle Paul had just survived a shipwreck after a fourteen-day storm. He was warming his hands in a fire on the island where he and the crew landed when a viper jumped out of the fire and bit him. When the people saw this, "they said among themselves, No doubt this man is a murderer, whom, though he hath escaped the sea, yet vengeance suffereth not to live" (v. 4, KJV).

This was Paul's test. The common belief was that a serpent would bite a person who should have died. And though Paul was among Gentiles, the rabbinical writings of that day attest to the fact that Jews also believed this. As soon as Paul came under attack, the people began to accuse him of wrongdoing.

Maybe you can relate to what Paul was going through. Perhaps some of your friends and family have been blaming you for the choices your children have made. If that is the case, I encourage you to follow Paul's example. The Bible says, "[Paul] shook off the small creature into the fire" (v. 5). As everyone looked on, Paul simply shook the viper off. He wasn't making a sideshow of himself. He wasn't trying to be a snake handler. He was just once again proving that God's Word is true, that "these signs shall follow them that believe . . . They shall take up serpents; and if they drink any deadly thing, it shall not hurt them" (Mark 16:17–18, KJV).

The locals knew this viper delivered a lethal bite. They wondered, "Would this stranger live or die?" But Paul sent the snake back to the fire where it belonged. Paul knew his purpose, and no snake was going to stop him from building God's kingdom. When people assail you with judgmental accusations, you have a choice to make. You can either take and nurture that offense or just shake it off.

We all face tests. How we react to those tests reveals our character. We may lose some battles, but we can win the war. Just get back up on your feet and try again. When 1 Corinthians 13:5 says love "takes no account of the evil done to it [it pays no attention to a suffered wrong]," it is saying that if you will walk in that kind of love, you will not keep track of the times people try to insult you. You may be aware of their attempts, but the love of God will be so strong around you that insults cannot penetrate the armor, and they won't bother you.

You cannot stop these verbal assaults from coming your way, but that doesn't mean you have to stand there and listen to them. You can leave the room or even the house until the person calms down enough for you to reason with him. You can not allow what they say to change your love for them, but you can do what Paul did—shake off these words and keep on going. Ask God to help you rise above your emotions, forgive those who have wronged you, and give you the strength and wisdom not to slight or avoid them or seek retaliation. Do as Paul did, and shake off that thing that is trying to distract you from your purpose.

The enemy fights hard to prevent that first breakthrough in your family because he knows if one person accepts the Lord, eventually all of them will. After Paul was bitten, the locals watched him as the crowd watches a matador at a bullfight. They observed his every move. Was he getting weaker from the bite? Would he die from the deadly venom? Did he deserve to die, as popular opinion would suggest? A severe viper bite can cause intense pain and swelling, difficulty breathing, and, depending on the type of snake, paralysis. If the person's body is not resistant to the effects of the venom or if there is no treatment, a viper bite can cause internal bleeding, kidney and respiratory failure, and ultimately death.[1] The locals waited, thinking Paul's death was imminent, but they just kept lingering until they realized this snake was not going to stop the apostle Paul.

This miracle changed their minds about him and made Paul something of a god in their minds. But God used that for his good. When he entered the foreign land of Italy from his native Israel, this display of God's power gave Paul tremendous credibility. Throughout the rest of Acts 28 we see how God opened doors for him to lay hands on the sick and perform the miraculous.

The test you may be going through today may actually be a doorway to the destiny God has for you. The author of two thirds of the New Testament may not have known all that God was going to do when he boarded the ship from Crete as a prisoner. But on the third day of the treacherous voyage from Crete, Paul told the ship's crew that "there will be no loss of life among you" (Acts 27:22). Fourteen days before the shipwreck and the salvation of the crew, Paul was already stating the outcome. He knew God had His hand on them.

Just as David defeated the lion and the bear as a boy, it gave him the confidence that God would give him victory over Goliath. In the same way Paul realized that this particular giant of a storm was not going to stop him.

Rejoicing in Hard Times

Sometimes when we are dealing with wayward relatives, judgmental friends and family, unforgiveness, bitterness, or even pride can try to latch onto us. But we cannot allow emotions to fester in our heart. Because the longer we let them linger, the worse those feelings become.

When we get happy in hard times, we are actually reflecting the heart of God himself. Even as the Bible says the joy of the Lord is our strength (Nehemiah 8:10). It tells us He who sits in the heavens laughs in derision at His enemies (Psalm 2:4) and that joy is inspired by the Holy Spirit (1 Thessalonians 1:6).

If you are sad all the time, you are not allowing the Holy Spirit to lead you. That can mean your flesh or the devil is driving you, and they definitely will do all they can to bring you into depression.

The Bible says God will turn your mourning into dancing. Anytime you are ready to give up, release the weight to Him. He has a joyful life planned for you. But because joy does not depend on what is going on around us, it has to be fired up from the inside.

The kingdom of heaven is righteousness, peace, and joy in the Holy Ghost (Romans 14:17). We are citizens of God's kingdom, not of this earth. If God can create and maintain innumerable galaxies of planets besides this earth, He can certainly turn the heart of a child from darkness to light. This is a completed work, like the healing, blessing, new life, and everything else Jesus accomplished through His death on the cross.

But ff you are doubting Thomas and have to see evidence of a turnaround before you believe, then victory will be a long time coming. Rejoicing on this side of the victory is a key ingredient to success. If prayer is the vehicle the Lord uses to bring victory, then praise is the highway.

The passage in 1 Thessalonians 1 referenced above says we are actually imitating Christ the moment we welcome His message, despite the persecution. When the Thessalonians rejoiced in God's Word in times of persecution, they became a "pattern to all the believers" (vv. 6–7). You may think, "Does God really want me to get happy when people are trying to hurt me?" That's what Jesus' disciples did, and their faithfulness continues to bear fruit to this day—every time the gospel is preached.

God Wars for Us

Psalm 68 says the righteous should be glad before God: "Let God arise, let his enemies be scattered: let them also that hate him flee before him. As smoke is driven away, so drive them away: as wax melteth before the fire, so let the wicked perish at the presence of God. But let the righteous be glad; let them rejoice before God: yea, let them exceedingly rejoice" (vv. 1–3, KJV). Why does the Bible say we should rejoice exceedingly before Him? Our praise is a mighty weapon in the hands of an almighty God. He can shut the mouths of our enemies and the accusers in our life. He is a personal God, and He knows your name, address, and social security number.

If we are children of God, we can be glad on that point alone. We were cleansed from sin by the blood of Jesus, and that made us righteous. The minute we become conscious of the presence of God, we can rejoice! "I will lift up my hands in Your name ... and my mouth shall praise You with joyful lips!" (Psalm 63:4–5). Psalm 27:6 says we are to "offer sacrifices and shouting of joy." Sometimes we just need to give Him the sacrifice of joy, thank Him for being strong for us when we feel weak.

God wants us to laugh in the face of the enemy. The devil will come after you and say, "What are you laughing about? You don't have anything to laugh about. God's not going to answer your prayer." But you can just remind the devil that Jesus already won the victory two thousand years ago. You are just declaring it in advance.

In Acts 27:25, when the boat Paul was traveling on was about to be shipwrecked, he told the other men, "So keep up your courage, men, for I have faith (complete confidence) in God that it will be exactly as it was told me." Paul was so confident because an angel had appeared to him and already told him that everything was going to be OK. Likewise, God has spoken to us through His Word and promised us that He wins in the end. We have a lot to be happy about.

JOY UNSPEAKABLE

Most people do not really cheer up when they're facing a storm. They go on the defense. They resign thenselves to thoughts like, "I am in a fight of faith right now. Don't bother me!" We cannot look as if we've lost the fight. We have to act as if we have won—because we have! Count it all joy. When? When we're facing any kind of trouble. Why? Because the trying of our faith brings patience (James 1:3).

If you say, "I'm going to wait until I feel happy to rejoice," you might be sitting there awhile. You don't feel your way into better action. You believe your way into better feeling. Shouting unto God and praising Him will produce the feelings of joy and thankfulness.

If we don't rejoice, the devil will think he is winning. If he sees us sad and weak, he knows that is the time to send in reinforcements and make us unhappier. But when we start to rejoice, it will cause the enemy to be still (Psalm 8:2; 9:2–4).

There are plenty of issues going on in your family, including our kids' rebellion, to bring us down. But cranking up our joy level is our best defense. Some people think they are being more spiritual when they refuse to laugh in the middle of a trial. But as I stated previously, God sits up in the heaven and laughs at His enemies (Psalm 2:4). After he lost his children and his worldly possessions, Job was told to laugh at famine and destruction (Job 5:22). Smith Wigglesworth, the famous twentieth-century British evangelist, said, "Faith laughs at impossibilities."[2]

First Peter 1:8 says, "Yet believing, ye rejoice with joy unspeakable and full of glory" (KJV). Joy unspeakable is unexplainable joy! No matter where we are geographically, people can look at us and know we have joy. This ushers in the glory of God and changes us. I've heard people say, "I've been praying. I've been with the Lord." But they still look sad. When we spend time with the Lord, His joy and peace will show on our faces.

Count it all joy! If we knew what happens in the Spirit when we rejoice, we would praise Him every day. Something happens when we laugh at impossibilities. This joy unspeakable is a heavenly, triumphant joy. If the devil can keep us sad, whining, and complaining, he has us boxed in a corner. But when we give God a shout of praise, we break those chains.

CHAPTER 12

Joy Defeats Darkness

IT WASN'T UNTIL I started laughing in the middle of a bad time, when things looked impossible, that I sensed a new freedom in my life. Laughter brings a supernatural release in your life that cannot be found in any other emotion. Laughing made me realize that even though I can't do anything about the situation, I underscore my trust in God when I choose to rejoice. Rejoicing is really another way of casting all your cares on Him.

The forces of darkness have to submit to the power of joy. Rejoicing is the ultimate antibiotic to your problem, the *über* penicillin for your situation. Satan's primary weapon is unleashing accusations against the children of God. But Psalm 8:2 says praise silences the avenger. Some translations use the word *stills* instead of *silences*. Rejoicing in God stops the devil and his minions in their tracks.

There is power in rejoicing. It is a force. This is why it is so important that you praise God in the middle of a hard time. It is not just because praising and thanking God make you feel better. It's because you are actually taking authority over the enemy the moment you start to praise.

Wherever Jesus ministered, the people He touched always

left filled with joy. They were set free and blessed, even though the critics and religious leaders mocked and scorned them. Who would not be happy to be healed and delivered of something oppressive, even if people were criticizing the Man who made it possible?

The same thing happens today. We might receive a miraculous answer to prayer, but the enemy will make sure there are people out there to undermine what God has done and claim it was just chance or good fortune. Instead of yielding to intimidation when you are under fire, rejoice, knowing heaven is celebrating your victory (Luke 10:20).

The powers of darkness must legally submit to the power of joy, but you cannot expect the enemy to be happy about it. We are invading his territory when we yield to supernatural joy. Joy overpowers sorrow, like a prize fighter knocking out his opponent in the first round of a championship match.

GOD WILL RESTORE

Several months after he committed adultery with Bathsheba and had her husband killed in battle, King David was sitting on his throne, trying to figure out why he was so miserable. He had lost his joy, but he didn't realize why until the prophet Nathan came and pointed it out to him. Sin is missing the mark. It will throw us off our game and cause us to live in the past, tormented by guilt and shame. David chose not to stay there. He acknowledged his wrongdoing and cried out to God in heartfelt repentance, "Restore unto me the joy of thy salvation" (Psalm 51:12, KJV). And the Lord answered him.

God will do the same for us when we cry out to Him to restore our joy. Perhaps you have been blaming yourself because your children have not arrived to where the Lord wants them. Perhaps you have given in to the lie that your family's situation will never change.

If you have lost your joy, if you are in the deepest depression you have ever known in your lifetime, thank God the sorrow does not have to be permanent! It is only seasonal. Winter turns to spring, spring to summer, then to fall. But it continues to change and so will your circumstances. Ask God to forgive you for holding your own pity party, and start praising Him even when your feelings disagree. The spirit of joy will rain down on you like a waterfall.. God is in the redemption business.

Right after college, I moved to England. Through a series of opportunities I became an antiques dealer in the Midlands. My business involved buying items at auctions and from private homes and shipping them to the United States to sell at auction. One day in my travels, I came across a real gem in an eighteenth-century Chippendale desk. It was completely original with ball and claw feet. It was the genuine article, but it needed serious restoration.

At one time the piece's rare patina had been clumsily painted over. But a trained eye could still see the original wooden dowels, as well as the irregular handwork and fine shaping of an authentic antique. It was obviously a collectible piece of furniture worth reviving. Even the pastel blue paint could not disguise the desk's remarkable value.

As much as you might see your children being painted over the original treasure that they are, the Father is always there ready to take that varnish off. But their willingness to return to Him might largely depend on how you handle yourself. Your children know when they are off course. Their flesh may be screaming at them, telling them what they are fine, but all the while the Spirit of God is gently and lovingly wooing them back to Him.

Our role as parents is to encourage them with as much of God's love as they can receive at one time. Children need to know your door is always open. They need to have confidence that when they do return, there is a place waiting for them at your table. They want to be assured that you have room for them in your heart and will not keep bringing up the past.

No matter how bad the situation may seem, never give up. "The king's heart is in the hand of the LORD, as the rivers of water: he turneth it whithersoever he will" (Proverbs 21:1, KJV). God alone can move the rudder of a person's heart. You never know when that heart will turn around, but you can stay ready and be expecting. You can prepare a child's heart with your love, but it is the Holy Spirit who ultimately will draw that child back to Himself.

In Luke 15, the father of the prodigal son waited on the porch with his arms open and set a table for joyful feasting once the son arrived. He was not mournful and judgmental. He did not make his son sleep with the pigs when he finally came home, even though that's what the wayward son thought he deserved after having spent all of his inheritance on wild living. The father celebrated his son's homecoming and pulled out all the stops. That patient and expectant father was the real hero of the story. He did not give up on his son, no matter how humiliated he may have felt.

People know when they are living off track. In fact they are so aware of it, they may begin to think they can never come back to God, that there is no hope for them. These feelings of unworthiness can become a real stumbling block if they don't experience unconditional love. Their pride and unbelief may be keeping them from admitting they want to change. But your love and forgiveness can open them up to hearing the truth and returning to the Lord.

When the son came to his senses, he knew where to go and what to do. The father maintained a humble heart and loved his son unconditionally. He yearned to receive his son back. That's a good thing, too. If the father had greeted the son with judgment and recrimination, the son probably would have turned around and jumped back into the world.

It was the jealous (and religious) elder brother who was scornful and couldn't figure out why his younger brother's return home was being celebrated after all he had put the family through. The bottom line was that the older son didn't understand why he did not get the same treatment for being loyal.

The father in that parable also loved this older son, and I believe he told him something like this:"Listen, you have always had access to everything I own.You never died.Your brother died (spiritually), and now he has come back to life.We need to be deeply grateful and rejoice in what God has done for him."

The Lord loves to restore backsliders. He is married to them.

He will not let them go. He can bring them back from wherever they are—no pit is too deep. Their hearts will soften toward the truth as we walk in humility before them and love them consistently and unconditionally.

TRIALS TEST OUR FAITH

There's no doubt that there will be trials and tribulations in our family. No one is exempt. But when we are traveling this road, we cannot afford to yield to hopelessness, despair, and depression. Replace them with what the Father has for you—love, joy, and peace. James 1:2 says there is only one way to deal with any difficult family situation—by counting it all joy. The word *count* in that verse actually means to command or to lead. In other words, holding onto joy will lead you out of the trial you find yourself in. And the length of time it takes you to go through that test totally depends on how long you keep yourself operating in the dark.

First Peter 1:7–9 tells us that the trials we go through test our faith.

> *So that [the genuineness] of your faith may be tested, [your faith] which is infinitely more precious than the perishable gold which is tested and purified by fire. [This proving of your faith is intended] to redound to [your] praise and glory and honor when Jesus Christ (the Messiah, the Anointed One) is revealed. Without having seen Him, you love Him; though you do not [even] now see Him, you believe in Him and exult and thrill with inexpressible and glorious (triumphant, heavenly) joy. [At the same time] you receive the result (outcome, consummation) of your faith, the salvation of your souls.*

Paul and Silas knew this and started to praise God at midnight in a filthy, dank prison cell, with a sentence of death in the morning hanging over their heads. Their praise was their warfare. It was the only weapon they had, and it worked. Their voices released their breakthrough. They exercised the power of joy in very difficult circumstances. Despite the fact that they had done nothing wrong, they were beaten with rods and thrown into a sewage and vermin-filled pit. In this depressing atmosphere, they fought against despair by singing and praising God.

Their response could only be supernatural because there was no way they would have felt like singing in that environment. They had nothing in the natural to be happy about. You may not either. You might be in the "dark night of the soul." But the soul is your mind, will and emotions. But it is your spirit that moves in whatever direction you point it to, whether that is your feelings or the Word. He is always with you if you are willing to listen. You are never alone, whether you realize it or not. God never leaves or forsakes you.

Because Paul and Silas made a decision to praise, "suddenly there was a great earthquake, so that the very foundations of the prison were shaken; and at once all the doors were opened and everyone's shackles were unfastened" (Acts 16:26). Now, you know it had to be the intervention of God for an earthquake to unlock prison doors. Those were high steel bars, impenetrable without a key to the lock. The Lord obviously loved their display of faith in overwhelming circumstances. And why not? Every time you open your mouth to magnify Him, you are releasing God's presence. He lives in your praise.

The joy of these determined disciples preceded their breakthrough. They were set free at dawn. Even their jailor was saved when he saw this miracle. I am convinced more people would turn to Jesus if they could see some Christians who were joyful in the middle of the fire. Isaiah 41:10 says God will "strengthen and harden you to difficulties." It is when you can praise God right in the middle of the flames that you see a release in your situation.

When Paul and Silas praised, the literal power of God shook the prison and broke all the prisoners' chains. We may have been shackled by our own thoughts, unforgiveness, bitterness, or hard-heartedness. We may have had thoughts such as, "All the years I have prayed and sought the Lord for this family, and now *this*? Can things get any worse?" But start releasing thanks in advance for your children's salvation, and watch Him break *all* strongholds that have been holding them—and you—hostage.

People spend so much money on psychiatrists, psychologists, mood-altering drugs, hypnosis, alcohol, and so on when a good session of worship can dispel the darkness. They are dealing with the soul while their spirits are starving. Natural and chemical remedies manage unhealthy thoughts and emotions temporarily, but they don't bring permanent healing. We are primarily and eternally a *pneuma*, or spirit. Our spirits will live forever. We also have a soul, which consists of our mind, our will, and our emotions. Our soul and spirit are housed in our bodies. Put simply, your spirit is that which knows (1 Corinthians 2:11), and the soul is that which feels (Job 14:22).

What we have been talking about throughout this book is a

joy that comes out of our inner man, not from our souls or our bodies. The only place we will find this refreshing is in Christ. We do not find it by seeing a therapist twice a week or taking Prozac. God certainly uses medical professionals to help us when we face mental health problems, but the joy of the Lord does more than manage the problem; it overtakes it.

After being beaten three times with rods, then being stoned once, and enduring three shipwrecks, Paul said, "Rejoice in the Lord always [delight, gladden yourselves in Him]; again I say, Rejoice!" (Philippians 4:4). Paul knew that joy is more than an attitude; it is the AK-47 that drives away the darkness.

Later in the seventies, I also had the opportunity to live on a macadamia nut farm in Rhodesia (now the country called Zimbabwe). Everyone on our compound was aware of terrorists who climbed up the mountains from Mozambique to kill and maim the farmers on the surrounding tea plantations. All night long, powerful quartz halogen lights laced the barbed-wire fence around our house, flooding the grounds with light. The strong beams from the huge searchlights made it obvious to potential invaders that we were on our guard and were not going to be easy targets. These lights provided protection for us in what could have been a deadly situation, as it did turn into years later when terrorists took over the country. Fortunately by that time, I had returned home to California.

Joy is like those halogen lights. It shows the enemy that we're not going to be easy targets. It creates a defense around us and illuminates the way so we can begin to see our children as God sees them. God laughs at His enemies, because He knows there is a reward on the other side of the trial.

When you start to separate spirits from a person and realize the issue is not with a human being but a supernatural demonic entity, it makes your perspective a lot clearer.

People are watching you walk through the valley you are in. They are wanting to see how you deal with it. The attitude of gratitude you display is a witness to others of God's goodness. He wants not only our children worshiping Him, but so many others as well. When we start getting excited about praying for and leading other people to the Lord, we will see our loved ones start to come in. As you take care of God's business, He takes care of yours.

Find another family who needs your prayers. Look for people you can turn into trophies for God while you are waiting for yours to return to Him. Job, who suffered so much loss, finally made the ultimate turnaround in chapter 42 when he prayed for his friends. God restored all that Job had possessed before his trial—his health, his children, and double his wealth.

Listen for the Holy Spirit to quicken you to pray for the children of your friends or other children He may lay on your heart. A woman's friend began praying for her daughter, who was waffling between staying with her lover and getting right with God. In the end, that friend's prayers made the difference. The girl moved from one state to another and went home to live with her parents. Other struggles ensued, but the prayer continued and the enemy was defeated.

I know I would not be serving the Lord today if not for my first-grade teacher, a Baptist lady who prayed daily for the salvation of everyone in my class. Although her prayers weren't answered until twenty-three years later, she sowed powerful seeds into my life that eventually brought forth fruit.

Joyful Parent

CHAPTER 13

Reap in Joy

THERE'S NO DOUBT weeping is going to come when children take a different path. But when the tears come, remember that joy is next up on the hit parade. You have to keep looking forward, visualizing the way God sees your child.

> *When the Lord brought back the captives [who returned] to Zion, we were like those who dream [it seemed so unreal] . . . . They who sow in tears shall reap in joy and singing. He who goes forth bearing seed and weeping . . . shall doubtless come again with rejoicing, bringing his sheaves with him.*
>
> —PSALM 126:1, 5–6

You may have been sowing seeds of mourning, but God guarantees the day will come when you will start to reap in joy and rejoicing. And what you release is going to blossom and form into sheaves. Sheaves (notice the plural form here) are not just a single stalk of grain resulting from one tiny seed but a whole head of wheat tied together into a sheaf. So what you've sown in tears does not produce just *one* sheaf but *many* sheaves—lots of joy, dancing, rejoicing, and happiness! Start meditating on that instead of what you are going through.

God wants to turn our mourning into dancing, but a religious mind-set will quench what He wants to do every time. We have to guard against becoming like the Pharisees, who were more concerned about outward signs of holiness than whether their hearts were right before God.

Jesus always offended people who tried to fit God into a neat little box, who put more stock in outward religious displays than on true repentance. In Matthew 15, knowing Pharisees were listening nearby, Jesus told a crowd, "It is not what goes into the mouth of a man that makes him unclean and defiled, but what comes out of the mouth" (v. 11). After He said this, His disciples asked Him, "Do You know that the Pharisees were displeased and offended and indignant when they heard this saying?" (v. 12).

Jesus responded, "Let them alone and disregard them; they are blind guides and teachers. And if a blind man leads a blind man, both will fall into a ditch" (v. 14). We often reject genuine moves of God because we are so caught up with rigid mental attitudes and religious strongholds. You can not judge everything that is going on around you mentally you have to start hearing what the Holy Spirit is saying to you about the situation. Naturally the Word and the Spirit must agree, and there are definitely people who falsely claim the Holy Spirit is leading them. But you will learn how to discern what is truly of God as you study the Word.

No one besides your own family wants to be like you if you are religious, legalistic, and boring. Jesus was not sent into this world to bind us up but to set us free, and He whom the Son sets free is free indeed. I have had firsthand experience with being religious and legalistic. I will choose a relationship with God that is joyful and happy, one that is dependent on hearing God's voice, over legalism any day.

I still regret not allowing our son to play Pop Warner football because many practices were held on Wednesdays. My husband and I were pastors of a church at that time, and our midweek services were held on that day. Even though there was not much for his age group to do that night, we thought he should be at church every time the doors were open. I thank God that my son continues to serve the Lord today as a leader and didn't let situations like that deter him from the call of God on his life. My religious mind-set at the time could have turned him off to church completely.

Be more concerned about what God thinks about you than about people's opinions of you. Don't fear man, but worship God.

PUT YOUR CONFIDENCE IN GOD

In Psalm 118:5, the psalmist talks about calling on the Lord in his distress. But I find it interesting that he doesn't ask God for anything until after he worshiped and thanked Him for having the very attributes he was asking Him to display in the distressing situation. He said, "The Lord is on my side: I will not fear. What can man do to me?" (v. 6). Then he acknowledges that the Lord lights him up with "grace, freedom, and joy" (v. 27). Here again, joy is lighting up the whole situation. Start to rejoice, and the situation will begin to change.

I know you may be wondering, "How long do I have to hold on?" Bear in mind that this is a spiritual battle. But like the angel said in the Book of Daniel, your prayer was heard the first day you prayed. But just like an orchestra has to practice for week to get ready to hold a concert, the Holy Spirit has to get everyone into position to get the battle won. What that verse does say is that the Prince of Persia opposed the angel, and there was a battle going on in the heavenlies.

Do your best to keep all lines of communication open. You want to give your child every reason to believe that you still love him, enjoy his company, and have confidence in his future. But take heart. Even God, the perfect Father, is not panicking, or beating Himself up. You do not need to either.

Having faith is simply having confidence in God. When we are trusting in His promises for household salvation, we can be assured that if God says He will do something, He will do it. Our heavenly Father promises that our children will return from the land of the enemy (Jeremiah 31:16–17), you and your entire household shall be saved (Acts 16:31), and your sons and daughters shall prophesy (Acts 2:17). You can rest assured that God's power is greater than the power of the enemy over your children. If He can turn the hearts of kings, He can draw your children back to Himself.

Faith comes out of rest; it does not come when you worry and expend a lot of energy. There are only two things that can stop your faith. The first is when you don't feed it with God's Word, and the second is when you allow doubt and unbelief to creep in and stop you from believing the Word. If you don't mix God's promises with your faith, you can become bitter because you don't see the answer, instead of better.

Resting *and* rejoicing in God's promises is the key to receiving. You can rest all you want, but if you are still worrying, you are all twisted up and unable to receive. If you don't rejoice, relax, and laugh once in a while, you will get so uptight you'll just snap. Cement is just dust until it gets mixed with water. Once it does, though, you had better get it poured quickly, because it will harden on you and be impossible to use. Your attitude can harden in the same way when you don't rest and rejoice in the Word. That's why you have to pour the oil of joy into your faith engine to get your motor moving again.

Hebrews 4:1–3 says, "We received the same promises as those people in the wilderness, but the promises didn't do them a bit of good because they didn't receive the promises with faith. If we believe, though, we'll experience that state of resting. But not if we don't have faith" (THE MESSAGE). You have to nurture your faith even when the cards seem to be stacked against you. How is that possible? When life starts to frustrate or upset you, ask yourself if you really believe the promises God gave you in His Word. I have particular scriptures the Lord has illuminated to me about each of our children. The only way you can stay away from tormenting spirits is to anchor yourself in what He is saying to you—and then apply it. You are always secure standing on a word the Lord has personally quickened in your spirit. Your real life is what is happening within you, where Christ lives, not in the people and circumstances around you. It is up to you to dig deeper.

You can rest assured that you are not alone in your trial. Jesus understands what you are going through. He is not a far-off, impersonal God. He is right here with you, this very moment, even though you can't see or feel Him. When you open the Word and start to read it, He will start to speak to you. His Holy Spirit will supernaturally direct you to scriptures relating to your situation.

He knows what has happened to you and with your children. He knows what you have been through. He experienced everything— every emotion and sorrow you feel, except He experienced it without sinning. He did not yield to feelings that are fickle and constantly changing. Jesus spent the first thirty years of His life studying the Word and letting it saturate His heart and mind before He started His three and a half years of ministry on earth. He prepared Himself for the onslaught of temptation He would face, and it is the Word that will prepare us for the battle as well.

You and I will never be able to say no to our feelings unless we have a strong imprint of God's Word in our hearts. Jesus had the same feelings you have, but He never succumbed to them because the Word of God in Him was stronger than the situation around Him. When your children hurt or upset you, go into a private place, lift your hands, and thank God for giving you wisdom and understanding at that moment.

God does not condemn you for hurt feelings. You need to tell Him you are glad He understands what you are going through and that you realize He never condemns you. The enemy is the one who will try to heap shame and regret on you. That's why the Bible calls Satan the accuser of the brethren. Don't sign for that package.

Return to sender, address unknown.

GOD'S NEW BEGINNINGS

Psalm 68 says, "God is [already] beginning to arise, and His enemies to scatter; let them also who hate Him flee before Him! . . . But let the [uncompromisingly] righteous be glad; let them be in high spirits and glory before God, yes, let them [jubilantly] rejoice! Sing to God, sing praises to His name, cast up a highway before Him Who rides through the deserts—His name is the Lord—be in high spirits and glory before Him!" (vv. 1, 3–4).

Our praise makes a path for the Lord to ride in on the deserts of our situation. He inhabits the praise of His people, but He can actively *move* when we are praising Him. If we want our prayers answered, we have to make a *way* for Him in our worship. We can't sulk or sorrow over our situation; mourning may endure for a night, we can be sorry for one night (for one period of time), but joy comes in the morning (Psalm 30:5).

You will sow in tears, but you will reap in *joy* and singing (Psalm 126:1, 5–6). So it is vital that you immerse yourself in the joy realm, whatever it takes. That is where your manifestation is going to show up. After all, God rejoices—He literally "spins around" in joy over you (Zephaniah 3:17). He delights in you and promises to take care of the shame, blame, or disgrace you may feel as you start to delight in Him. He is planning to reverse your captivity right before your eyes!

God is not going to take back what He gave you. He has said

He certainly will bless you, and in multiplying, He will multiply you (Hebrews 6:14).

Jesus is the Lion of the tribe of Judah—the tribe of praise. When a lion roars, it can be heard miles away. He puts his head down and roars into the ground, and the ground thunders. The lion marks his territory! As followers of Christ, we too are lions of Judah. We must lay out our territory with praise and put the enemy on notice. Satan is stopped in his tracks when we praise God.

In 2 Chronicles 20, the people of Moab, Ammon, and Mount Seir rose up to fight against the people of Judah. When King Jehoshaphat learned that a great army was coming against him, fear immediately set in. But he didn't stay there, paralyzed. He called a fast throughout the cities of Judah, and they sought the Lord.

Then the Spirit of the LORD came upon Jahaziel the son of Zechariah, the son of Benaiah, the son of Jeiel, the son of Mattaniah, a Levite of the sons of Asaph, in the midst of the assembly. And he said, "Listen, all you of Judah and you inhabitants of Jerusalem, and you, King Jehoshaphat! Thus says the LORD to you: 'Do not be afraid nor dismayed because of this great multitude, for the battle is not yours, but God's. Tomorrow go down against them. They will surely come up by the Ascent of Ziz, and you will find them at the end of the brook before the Wilderness of Jeruel. You will not need to fight in this battle. Position yourselves, stand still and see the salvation of the LORD, who is with you, O Judah and

Jerusalem!' Do not fear or be dismayed; tomorrow go out against them, for the LORD *is with you."*

—2 CHRONICLES 20:14–17, NKJV

With that promise from the Lord, Jehoshaphat led the people in worshiping God. Notice that their enemies were still lined up to attack. Jehoshaphat praised God based on His promise to deliver the people. When they rose early in the morning to go out to battle, Jehoshaphat told the people, "Believe in the LORD your God, and you shall be established; believe His prophets, and you shall prosper" (v. 20, NKJV). He was telling them that God could be trusted, no matter how bad the circumstances seemed. Then he called on those who could sing and praise God to go out into the battle before the rest of the army. "As they went out before the army and were saying: 'Praise the LORD, for His mercy endures forever'" (v. 21, NKJV).

The Bible says when they began to sing, the Lord set ambushes against the armies that rose up against the people of Judah. The people of Ammon and Moab turned on the army from Mount Seir; then when Mount Seir was destroyed, the Ammonites and Moabites turned on each other. When the people of Judah looked toward the army, all they saw were dead bodies. No one escaped.

Just as King Jehosephat sent the praisers to the front of the battle lines, God wants us to put praise first when we face our battles. If we do, we will see the victory just as the Israelites did. The Bible says, "Arise and thresh, O Daughter of Zion!" (Micah 4:13).

In other words, no matter what we're facing, we have to get up and get going. You will not win any battles standing still. When the Bible says, "Where there is no vision, the people perish" (Proverbs 29:18), it literally means, "My people cast off restraints!" You must maintain a vision for your children's salvation, no matter what state they are currently in.

Getting a new vision in her heart worked for the woman in Korea whose daughter was a prostitute. It worked for the woman whose daughter lay in a coma with no expectations to live and for the mother whose son was out of control. We have to change what we see, what we say, and what we believe about our children.

We can't wait on the answer to begin to praise, rejoice, and sing. When we praise Him in advance, we are demonstrating to God that we believe Him before we see the victory. This is faith—it is the substance of things hoped for, the evidence of things not seen (Hebrews 11:1). We have to look higher. We need to be *joyful* parents—not defeated ones—before the battle, during the battle, and after the victory.

CHAPTER 14

Rest and Rejoice

THERE'S REAL VICTORY in being able to cast the care of our children's salvation onto the Lord. But what happens in our hearts after that? What happens to our attitudes? We have to trust God to the point where we can rejoice and relax as if we already see His life in them.

First Thessalonians 3:7–8 says, "Brethren, for this reason, in [spite of all] our stress and crushing difficulties we have been filled with comfort and cheer about you [because of] your faith (the leaning of your whole personality on God in complete trust and confidence). Because now we [really] live, if you stand [firm] in the Lord."

If you want to maintain strong and resilient faith, you have to let it go. Otherwise you get all wound up and brittle, thinking your children's transformation depends on your efforts. That is a clear sign that you're not trusting God and His Word. We each choose whether to rest in God and be filled with His joy and laughter or to worry and fret.

One reason people turn away from God during tough times is because they have never learned how to speak the way God thinks and line their words up with His will. Walking through a trial is discouraging enough, but when you start telling all your friends about it and making the circumstances look so bad that only the devil can win, it can really bring everyone around you down. And they believe your negative report, which only reinforces it. You depress everyone around you (including yourself) with negative speech. That is why it is so important to align your conversation with God's will and His Word. When you saturate yourself in God's Word, it will become the rudder of your life and your tongue and will turn your life in the direction God desires for you.

A faith conversation always agrees with what the Word says. If you are really believing for your son to turn around, you don't pray for his salvation then tell your best friend at dinner that night, "I am so afraid my son is going to go down the wrong path and ruin his life." A parent who is really standing in faith for a child will say, "I am so blessed that God is working in my son's life, and he is going to fulfill the plan the Lord has for his life." You might be waiting and waiting for your child to turn around, but not with the right mindset. Adjust what you are thinking and saying and expect your child to line up with God's will for his life; start declaring and decreeing your expectations. Your hope and expectancy will pave the way for your miracle.

I know a young girl whose attitude turned around completely after her parents aligned their conversation with the Bible. Shannon has come full circle through prayer and praise. Her parents, former pastors and now evangelists, refused to let her go. It was not an easy journey. Shannon shares her story in her own words.

High school is where I started looking for freedom in all the wrong ways. After growing up in the church, I started to feel suffocated by it and my parents' rules. It was enough to make me abandon my values and walk the path that lured me in so easily. I was looking for freedom in partying and love from new relationships and friendships. A life without God skewed my values system but never fulfilled me.

Throughout the summer of my sophomore year of high school, I ended up in the emergency room on quite a few occasions. One time was due to alcohol poisoning; another was a very close call after I consumed one too many capfuls of the date rape drug GHB. Yes, I knew exactly what I was getting myself into, and it almost cost me my life.

After my close encounters with death, I continued to party and drink, which led to a bad fall that caused temporary nerve damage and brought on convulsions. My parents had then decided to send me to the opposite end of California to live with my no-nonsense aunt. That move and many prayers saved my life.

After high school, I mellowed out a bit but still was having my share of nights out at the bars and bad relationships. I craved love, but in all the wrong places. I had a good upbringing with parents who loved me, but the addictive lifestyle I was living left me empty and consistently brokenhearted. I would return to the Lord here and there but would also get sucked back into the worldly, superficial cesspool. I didn't find God fun; I thought getting drunk was fun at the time. It was when I was twenty-five years old that things began to change spiritually for me.

I remember one night I had a dream that my parents had given me some money to do something fun. I opened the door to leave our house, but as I stepped out, it became dark, and I found myself walking down some stairs. As I looked all around me, there were different levels of stairs, and as I stood on something like a bridge, feeling lost, giant flames rose up on both sides of me. I instantly felt a dark, evil presence around me and was overcome by fear. I turned around, but only darkness surrounded me. I desperately wanted to find home and asked God to help me. Suddenly I heard faint voices. The voices were those of my parents praying. I began to follow the prayers until they got louder and louder, and they eventually led me home.

This dream was quite powerful, and I knew I needed to make a change, but a part of me wasn't hungry enough for the things of God or the lifestyle I thought would come with it. Would I have to give up who I am to follow God? What if I got bored? As these questions weighed heavily on me, I eventually started noticing my desire to party and get involved with the wrong guys begin to fade. It was becoming easier to refuse the lifestyle I seemed to feel stuck in. God was doing something special inside of me, and although I did have to make tough choices, the inner battle seemed to get easier.

It was July of 2010, and I was getting my life together. I had been single and out of bad relationships for close to four years, but one night in July everything changed. Even though I was in a better place in my life, I still felt a void inside at times. One night, I remember lying in bed just sobbing. I felt like I had called out for Jesus and prayed for things without really having any answers. I felt angry and sad all at the same time. Out of desperation I said, "God, if You can hear me, I need You more than ever. I need You to fix this emptiness and help me. If You hear me, then I ask that You do something tomorrow morning when I wake up."

I cried myself to sleep but woke up singing a different tune. The moment I opened my eyes, I felt so overwhelmed by God's love that it brought tears of joy. I knew something so drastic had happened inside of me that only God could could have done it. Some of the first revelation was found in the Book of James. I had forgotten James was even a book in the Bible, but God knew it was exactly what I needed to read for encouragement. It was all about having faith and persevering through trials.

From that day on I rededicated my life, and especially through worship, I have found God's goodness in every situation. That same year, God brought me my precious husband. But God had been preparing him for me and me for him. In His perfect timing, everything came together like a rushing wind. The day I surrendered was the day my life changed. I have had more fun and more freedom to be me than I have ever had before![1]

Shannon's parents are friends of ours, and we saw them stand in faith for her return to the Lord. I asked Shannon's mom, Alice, to describe her daughter's turnaround from a mother's point of view, because I believe it will encourage those of you who may be growing weary.

There was a point at which I realized our daughter's lifestyle and choices were out of our hands. There was nothing we could do except to surrender her and lay her at the feet of Jesus. We had to relinquish control, but not care of her. We began to tell her, "Shannon, we may not agree with your choices, but we always accept and welcome you into our hearts and home. We love you first, not what you do."

Shannon was filled with the Holy Spirit at age three. I heard her singing in tongues one day as she was playing. She had already been saved and just wanted more of Jesus. She was very creative, loved to write stories, and loved to connect with people and help them. It was easy to see she was gifted and had a heart to help and bless others' lives from the start.

However, when she became a teenager, she chose worldly ways and relationships. She experimented with the party drug ecstasy, drank heavily, and lived a wild party life with friends. More than once, we were in the emergency room because of her choices. Once she hit her head hard on a friend's bathroom floor while she was drinking. Alcohol impairs your judgment and will make you do all kinds of crazy things. After that incident, she started having grand mal seizures and had to be put on medication for years afterward.

She then decided to become a blackjack dealer at a casino in northern California. At the same time, she entered into a very abusive relationship. This man had a violent temper, and one night he began choking her to the point that she feared for her life. That very night she packed her bags and made the nine-hour drive straight to our house. That night was also a turning point for Shannon and the beginning of us seeing answers to prayers we had prayed for so many years.

On the very same night Shannon drove home, we

were at a prophetic meeting in Carlsbad, California,at the opposite end of the state. We were listening to a prophet from Bethel Church in Redding,. The minister called out my husband and began prophesying to him. This prophet spoke a word to him about our daughter. He said she was in God's hands, that her Father really loved her, and that we should not worry. God had her and was holding her like a baby in His arms. As soon as we left the meeting, Shannon called, crying and screaming hysterically, and told us she was coming home because of the attack that night.

There were many steps along the way for her deliverance, but we continued to intercede and speak the Word and God's promises over her life, regardless of what we saw her doing. All through the years we prayed and interceded with groanings in the Spirit, calling out her name before God, speaking the promises of the Word over her. During this time my husband would faithfully take authority and break the power of ungodly relationships that Shannon would enter into, according to Psalm 129:4 and Isaiah 58:6, which speak of breaking ungodly ties. One by one these relationships would eventually break apart, or Shannon would lose interest in the guy.

We also reminded her of her worth and value. We kept telling her that God always had a greater destiny for her and someone who would love her the way He does. Many times the situation did not look good, and we wondered if we would ever see the fruit of our prayers. We were in a place of surrender, and we knew we had to give our daughter to the Lord and even release the dreams we felt God had for her life. We were in a place of totally trusting Him and believing that "[her] times are in [God's] hands" (Psalm 31:15).

Slowly Shannon was led to come back home again and stay with us. She began to read the Bible and pray again on her own. God began to visit Shannon with prophetic and spiritual warfare dreams and give her revelation. And she started to allow her heart to turn back to the One who calls her by name.

One of the dreams Shannon had was so significant and encouraging, testifying to the power of a parent's prayers. In it, her dad and I had given her some money to do with as she wanted —to go and have fun. She then went through a door and began going down some stairs. She was aware there were different levels of stairs around her, but she kept going down deeper and deeper on these stairs. She was aware of darkness, the presence of evil, and fire burning the farther down she went. It was a frightening place. When she turned to go back up the stairs and go through the door back to the light and to home, it was so dark she could not find the door.

Then she heard her dad and me praying in the background, very faintly at first. As she followed the sound of our intercession, the words on her behalf got louder and louder, and those prayers created a path for her to walk out of the darkness. They led her to the door she needed to go through!

Never give up on your prayers for your children; even though they may seem to fall on deaf ears sometimes, these prayers touch our children's spirits and lead them back to home! Parents' prayers do prevail! No matter what wrong turns and dead ends our children may take, our God is still so amazing and able to work it all out so they end up exactly where they were meant to be and become who God made them to be.

In 2010, we moved to be a part of a revival church in northern California. Within a matter of a few months Shannon met "the one," a wonderful man chosen of God, at a singles life group in the church. A few months later, they were married in the presence and blessing of the Lord and with the blessing of both parents and families!

The Lord's Word in Jeremiah 31:16–17 has come to pass: "For thy work shall be rewarded, saith the LORD; and they shall come again from the land of the enemy. And there is hope in thine end, saith the LORD, that thy children shall come again to their own border" (KJV). Selah.[2]

What a great testimony to the power of persistence! God's promises are the same yesterday, today, and forever (Hebrews 13:8). Just believe Him and rest in the fact that He is the Master Craftsman, and He is getting the job done as you cast the care of the situation on Him. We cannot play the role of the Holy Spirit in our children's lives. We should stop worrying about the outcome, because we know He has it all under control. Let God be true and every man a liar (Romans 3:4).

Lawyers base their legal arguments on old adjudicated trials that have set precedents. They depend on those previous verdicts to win current cases. As Christians, we do the same thing. We look to the Word of God as the precedent that determines what God will do in our current situation. Without these promises, we would not have a leg to stand on. But when He has quickened something to your hearts, it is as good as gold if you can hold onto it. If we pray according to that Word, we can expect future victory. The Word of God is more reliable than any case a lawyer may have won in a courtroom. It is an eternal contract with no expiration date.

JEREMIAH'S HOPE

Most of the choices prodigals make during this time in their lives stem from their desire to fill a void. Only God can meet that need, but as Shannon's story demonstrates, they have to figure that out for themselves. This is, again, why as believers our behavior is essential during this time of our children's lives, because we may be the only Bible they ever read to point them toward the truth. We can be the fertilizer, or the lack of it, for their progress or a hindrance to it.

Jesus said, "I am the Light of the world. He who follows Me will not be walking in the dark, but will have the Light which is Life" (John 8:12). False gods have no life. If we will pray, break the strongholds working in the lives of our unsaved loved ones, and thank God for bringing them to salvation, we will soon begin to see a change.

I challenge you to look for the good in your offspring. Your child may not be living for the Lord; he may be having substance abuse, or had brushes with the law. But no matter where your child is, you have something to be thankful for. You can be grateful that your child is alive and not hanging on the end of a snapped bungee cord somewhere. I encourage you to make an effort every day to look for something in your child's life to give God thanks for, even if it's the very breath they breathe.

God's compassion never ends. Lamentations 3:22 says, "It is

because of the Lord's mercy and loving-kindness that we are not consumed, because His [tender] compassions fail not." When Jeremiah wrote Lamentations, he focused only on his problems in the first two chapters and how his soul was bowed down with sorrow. But finally, in Lamentations 3, he began to see his life differently and started to focus on how good God had been to him. Sometimes we just need to stop focusing on ourselves and the problems we face and start recalling past victories in our lives. We can remind ourselves that God has been faithful to us before, and He will come through for us again.

We are not the be-all and end-all of the universe. God is. If we decide to concentrate on something outside ourselves, we will increase our ability to hope in God and expect His mercy in our situation. The shift in Jeremiah's mind-set pulled him out of the pit of depression and despair. When we change our mind-set from one that is introspective and negative to one that believes God's promises, we will move from glory to glory.

Jeremiah's hope in the Lord brought him out of the miserable state in which he found himself. When we constantly stew over problems, meditating and hashing them over in our minds, we sink deeper and deeper into despair. But thinking about the goodness and mercy of God will refocus us every single time.

PRAY IN THE SPIRIT

I cannot overstate how important it is to look to the Holy Spirit to guide us through problem situations. I have talked repeatedly about the power of prayer, but I want to specifically address the power of praying in the Spirit. When we pray in tongues, we allow the Holy Spirit to pray through us. There is so much we cannot know or understand about a situation, but the Holy Spirit knows, and when we pray in tongues, He gets right to the heart of the matter.

When we learn to yield to the leading of the Holy Spirit (as soon as we sense it and not later, long after we felt His prompting), we position ourselves to pray according to God's will. As we immerse ourselves in the Spirit and pray in other tongues, we begin to flow in His rest. We receive a supernatural joy that puts us on top of the problem instead of below it.

Several years ago after our son, David, graduated from Bible school, he wanted to go directly to Los Angeles to try his skills in acting. He had been precocious in comedy from a young age. When he was nine, he was watching Bill Cosby's show *Kids Say the Darndest Things* one afternoon and turned to me and said, "Mom, I want to be on that show." I thought to myself, *So do thousands of other young children.* But not wanting to discourage him, I said, "OK, David. I will call them."

Lo and behold, they let him come down to the studio and try out. He ended up making the producers laugh so hard, the camera people in the next room had to come in and tell them to be quiet because they couldn't film with all the background noise. He proceeded to go on the show not once but twice, and he later led his own comedy sports team in high school. Then in Bible school, he was head of the drama team, putting on skits for the school and the two-thousand-member church he attended.

I knew David was talented, but the idea of him going into secular drama after Bible school didn't sit right in my spirit. But I also knew it would do little good for me to tell that to a twenty-year-old. It was time to do some serious intercession, fasting, and praising. For five days, I laid David and his life out before the Lord, praying in the Spirit because I didn't know all God had planned for my son's future, but He sure did.

My husband stood in agreement with me, and we prayed together that God would have His way in our son's life. At the end of the week, David called us and said he had changed his mind. He decided he would rather join Teen Mania's Acquire the Fire acting team for a year, touring the nation and winning thousands of souls to Christ. It was not an easy year for him since the actors double as stagehands and do any and everything that needs to be done, sometimes living in grueling conditions on the road, but it was a very fruitful and maturing year for him.

CHANGE YOUR MIND-SET

In Psalm 143, King David was in the middle of a bad situation and could have allowed himself to be swallowed up in depression and despair. He had committed adultery with Bathsheba, another man's wife, and she became pregnant through the encounter. David then put her husband, Uriah, who was a dedicated soldier, at the front of a battle the Israelites were engaged in so he would be killed. When David's plan worked, he married Bathsheba, and their baby was born. (See 2 Samuel 11–12.)

However, the child became sick unto death. David fasted and prayed for the child, pleading with God to heal him, but all to no avail. The child died. Full of grief but knowing the baby was with the Lord, David made a choice about where he would set his mind. He said, "I remember the days of old; I meditate on all Your doings; I ponder the work of Your hands" (Psalm 143:5). David chose to remember how good God had been to him in the past, and he rejoiced and praised the Lord, choosing to repent and accept responsibility for his actions rather than blame God. His praise helped him avoid becoming bitter and depressed after the loss of his son.

David and Bathsheba had another son, whom they named Solomon. Solomon built the temple his father started and also wrote the Book of Proverbs. At one time he was believed to be the wisest man on earth, though he lacked common sense when he married women who did not share his faith. Because of the negative consequences of those unions, Solomon also wrote the Book of Ecclesiastes, which talks about his regrets and what is truly important in life.

What we think and meditate on plays an important role in our victory. The Holy Spirit speaks to us every time we open the Bible and begin to read it. But are we listening? Do we believe? Are we doing what He is telling us through the Scriptures?

Many people can recite whole passages of the Bible, but they've never learned to apply it to their lives. James 1:22 tells us to be doers of the Word and not hearers only. The Bible is a life-giving instruction book penned by the Spirit of God himself. We ignore what He is saying to our own peril. The key to victory with our children, or any other battle we face in our life, is in our mind-set. The key to breakthrough is lining that mind up with the Word of God. If we refuse to do this or think it's not important enough to prioritize, we will never experience victory.

King David understood the importance of praise. He knew he would experience a breakthrough from depression if he would just praise the Lord. So he lifted his hands in worship and said, "I spread forth my hands to You; my soul thirsts after You like a thirsty land [for water]. Selah [pause, and calmly think of that]!" (Psalm 143:6).

David told God he was desperate for Him. If you have reached a point of desperation, it is time to worship as never before. Worship moves God's heart. The Lord will do things for a worshiper He won't do for anyone else.

One thing I love about David is that he was transparent. He admitted that he had reached the end of his rope and needed God. A lot of times when people are depressed and desperate, they look for help in all the wrong places, making their problems worse. Only the Lord can quench a thirsty soul. He can completely satisfy and comfort anyone during a time of trial. He is the one who can turn things around.

COUNT IT ALL JOY

My husband, Keith, and I minister abroad several times a

year, and recently we found ourselves preaching in Medellín, Colombia. We are blessed to have open doors in this South American country, especially in this city that had been plagued by drug wars for decades. About eighteen years ago, drug kingpin Pablo Escobar lost his hold on the city and most of the country during a violent shootout that resulted in his death. But remnants of his organization remain in Medellín.

We found ourselves at the Rionegro Airport, located on top of a mountain some forty-five minutes above Medellín. We needed to exchange our money, so Keith and our trusted Colombian translator (an ex-drug dealer himself who was saved in a Miami prison) went to the exchange counter while I stood by the luggage. This was a necessary task in an airport rife with rings of thieves watching your every move.

I noticed an individual eying our four suitcases and box of books with way too much interest. This swarthy figure, who was wearing all black and a Russian proletariat cap to boot, gave me a sinister smile as he listened to someone on his cell phone. Apparently one of his colleagues from several rooms away was watching Keith and the translator exchange the money and they were relaying this information to this man.

Keith approached the baggage cart I was guarding and lifted my book bag to put his shoulder bag underneath. He then proceeded to roll the whole kit and caboodle out onto the sidewalk to look for a taxi. Jammed under my heavy book bag, this shoulder bag seemed to be impervious to theft, especially with Keith watching it. We rolled the luggage cart some twenty feet onto the sidewalk in the taxi waiting area, only to find a Prius-sized car the only transportation available to accommodate three people and our load of luggage.

The Colombian baggage handler ran around the taxi three times before he and Keith figured out how to systematically load the large cargo into the small car. Although no one actually saw what happened because it took place so quickly, the thief pilfered the small shoulder bag during the confusion.

The man in black, who had been so carefully inspecting me and my luggage, walked out to the sidewalk and stood beside me. I wondered the whole time why this man appeared so concerned about whether we got our luggage loaded into the taxi. Little did I realize the whole thing had been set up by a gang of thieves!

The swarthy thief moved next to my husband and our translator friend, who was busily overseeing the luggage loading with what we all thought was painstaking care. The black-clad assailant distracted us all with a big smile at the very moment the top book bag was being lifted into the trunk, exposing the shoulder bag beneath. No one actually saw what happened to the shoulder bag, because at the critical moment our eyes had been distracted.

As we drove away from the airport, Keith noticed his shoulder bag was missing. He looked everywhere, and it could not be found. For once in his life, he had put all his eggs in one basket. Both of our passports, his favorite Bible filled with notes, his iPhone with all his contacts, his iPad, cash, and his jewelry disappeared in an instant thanks to a ring of thieves operating with a Robin Hood mentality right before Christmas.

What were we supposed to do? Give in to despair and depression, or rejoice and relax? I can tell you resting in the Lord was *not* our first choice. We were scheduled to preach at a new church in Medellín that night but after the theft, that was the last thing we felt like doing. It was like Satan sucker punched us in the solar plexus. Encouraging others in the Lord was the last thing on our to-do list.

The pastors of that church came over to our hotel, prayed with us, and asked what they could do. Their graciousness gave us the fortitude to get up and get going again, so we mustered our strength and went off to the church. We decided that the best remedy was to give the enemy some of his own medicine and get people saved, healed, and delivered! And that's exactly what we did.

The next obstacle we faced was the dilemma of getting back to the United States without cash or our passports. Our pastor-friends kindly escorted us to the Medellín police station to file a police report of the theft. As we were sitting there, Keith opened a Bible the church had given him. Zechariah 8:3 spoke to him—"Thus says the Lord: I shall return to Zion and will dwell in the midst of Jerusalem, and Jerusalem shall be called the [faithful] City of Truth, and the mountain of the Lord of hosts, the Holy Mountain."

I shall return. The words reminded Keith of what God told the Israelites in Exodus 22:12 when He was establishing the law: "But if it is stolen when in his care, he shall make restitution to its owner." Keith sensed the Holy Spirit was telling him to keep on going, that he would recover all because the Lord was going to return it to him! A ray of hope lit up our hearts.

Even though we had to change our flights home and instead fly to Bogotá, the Colombian capital, to get new passports, the hand of God was with us all the way as we continued to trust in His goodness and restoration power. It turned out after a few calls to our family in the States, that one of our daughter's friends was a former Colombian national, and his uncle was once the president of Colombia. This friend contacted his aunt, who loaned us her bodyguards (the equivalent of America's Secret Service) for the day. They picked us up at the airport in an unmarked SUV, promptly dropped our luggage off at the hotel, and then took us to the American Embassy.

The first thing we saw was a mile-long line filled with Colombians applying for American work visas—not a promising sight! However, these savvy bodyguards had a better way. They drove us to the side of the embassy reserved for US citizens and moved us through the guard gate with their impressive credentials and diplomacy, and we ended up right in the middle of the lost passport office within ten minutes. We were so grateful for the goodness of God in a country where we hardly knew anyone and couldn't speak the language.

While sitting there in the embassy, we laughed with the passport officers who all spoke English, and explained our plight. We filled out all the passport forms and submitted our proof of identity. Then they said we could come back in two days to pick up our documents. But we continued to talk and lightly banter with them. All of a sudden, the passport officers decided they could process our passports that afternoon.

But a couple of minutes later, the officials looked around the room and saw that no one was there, which was a miracle in itself. So they said, "Just wait here. We can have it done in ten minutes!" We had new passports less than three hours after we arrived at the embassy. We celebrated by doing a jig right in the middle of the American Embassy passport office, to the chagrin of the officers looking on. Fortunately Colombians like to celebrate, so it didn't take long for the officers to lighten up and laugh.

We continued to thank God for restoring everything we lost, even when we could see no natural results. We continued to sow seed even when we were in lack. Within a week of the theft, we had the means to buy a new iPhone, complete with a cover and a free Blackberry for the ministry, and our shoulder bag was returned, though not much was left besides our keys and some old photographs. But through it all, we saw God's people pitch in to help, and in time God replaced everything that was lost with even better equipment. God responded miraculously when we chose to praise and trust Him.

CHAPTER 15

Wait on the Lord

THE BIBLE TELLS us one of the reasons trials come in the first place is to teach us patience. Paul prayed in 2 Thessalonians 3:5, "May the Lord direct your hearts into [realizing and showing] the love of God and into the steadfastness and patience of Christ and in waiting for His return." Patience is not just a matter of waiting; it is how we react while we are waiting. We must learn to wait with a good attitude.

You will never get out of waiting. You will wait in the doctor's office, the grocery store, the bank. We are always waiting for something. But it is *how* you wait that determines how long you are going to stay in that place and how pleasant the wait will be. You can make it miserable or enjoyable. It's your choice! You will spend more time waiting in life than receiving, so you might as well make it pleasant.

God is watching you as you wait. Psalm 33:18 says, "Behold, the Lord's eye is upon those who fear Him [who revere and worship Him with awe], who wait for Him and hope in His mercy and loving-kindness." And we read in Isaiah 40:31, "They that wait upon the LORD shall renew their strength; they shall mount up with wings as eagles; they shall run, and not be weary; and they shall walk, and not faint" (KJV).

The eagle is one of the strongest birds in the world. Its wingspan can reach as wide as eight feet, allowing it to catch the wind and glide high above the earth and close to the sun. These birds have long symbolized power and purpose, strong and manly piety, being elevated above the world, and flowing in communion with God.

When you take your problems to God, focusing on His goodness, mercy, and ability to deliver your child, you will gain new strength. You will feel a sense of renewed purpose to move forward in whatever situation you are facing. Sitting and staring at the current circumstance just causes you to "sit, soak, and sour." That is what my husband and I used to tell our congregation when we pastored years ago. If you don't receive what the Lord has spoken to your heart in this book, you will literally "stew in your own juices."

God is trying to tell you there is another way of looking at the situation you face. Getting a new perspective is how you are going to bring restoration and repair in your family. But you have to go up to Him and get rid of the old judgments and attitudes that may have pushed your offspring away from you. You have to shed the past, ride the wind of the Holy Spirit, and fly close to the Son.

While you are waiting, you can deal with hindering attitudes such as thinking, "Poor me," or, "Why does this always happen to me?" The enemy can jump in and wreak havoc in your mind with that one if you let him! I have found that it is best to let God be

God and learn patience while He works unhealthy attitudes out of me. I encourage you to do the same. You will enjoy the journey much better when you do. Spending time in the Word gets you off that emotional roller coaster and back onto solid ground.

The Word redirects your thought life. Old attitudes are transformed in the face of God's thoughts. Peace arises, and unforgiveness departs. Your stamina increases because you recognize the source of your problem: it is not a person but the spirit behind that person! "Great peace have they who love Your law; nothing shall offend them" (Psalm 119:165).

One sign of spiritual maturity is being able to live beyond your feelings. When you are waiting for the manifestation of what you've been praying for, you have to keep rejoicing if you want results. Preparing for God's best is a process, and anything that takes time will require waiting.

TAKING TROPHIES ALONG THE WAY

When you are waiting for your prayer to be answered, the great temptation is to give birth to an Ishmael, to do something in the natural to bring about the answer yourself. You can't force anyone to get saved. People can only accept the Lord when the Holy Spirit draws them. They have to take ownership of their own salvation for it to last for eternity.

Evangelist Billy Graham's ministry had a huge retention of converts in his meetings because he would have teams of people praying a year before his organization held a crusade in a city. Their prayers would till the ground so the seed of the gospel could take root in people's hearts. We can cooperate with the Holy Spirit—we *should* cooperate with the Holy Spirit—but He is the ultimate soulwinner. He is the one who draws people to repentance.

If you decide to forgo His leadings and choose to do it your way, then you will have to live with an Ishmael of a situation, just as Abraham did. At the root of the conflict in the Middle East is Abraham's decision to get ahead of God and try to fulfill the promise his way. The Arab and Jewish people—the children of Ishmael and the children of Isaac—continue to fight to this day over what their rightful inheritance is. "Let patience have her perfect work" while you wait, "that ye may be perfect and entire, wanting nothing" (James 1:4, KJV).

You know, an attack on your faith is merely an opportunity to prove that God is true and every man a liar. A trial tests your faith, and even though the test is not from God, you still must stand strong and remain in faith. A boxer loses his mettle if he does not work out every day. He has to be in the gym consistently if he expects to stay in shape and win the next fight.

A good boxer has the rhythm of a ballet dancer; his punches literally flow in perfect timing. But he doesn't jump in and start jabbing right away. He waits and studies his opponent to find out where his weakness is; then he goes in for a quick punch. Once his arm strikes a weak point on the challenger, he goes after the same area over and over again. When you hold up God's Word to the enemy and continue to praise God in the middle of a battle, you have located the devil's weakness. He cannot stand in the praises of God. Keep praising and keep declaring God's Word until you see the strongholds over your children come tumbling down.

As I've said before, the only way to last in a test is to "count it all joy when you fall into various trials" (James 1:2, NKJV). James, the half-brother of Jesus, is telling us in this verse that we will have trials that catch us off guard—circumstances that are the last thing you would ever expect to happen in your family. No one in this life is immune to tests; the enemy will see to that. Yet when you react to the situation with laughter instead of sorrow, knowing the Lord *will* answer, you are turning the tables on the devil and positioning yourself to win.

Consider the annual Ironman Triathlon that has been held in Hawaii for more than three decades. This feat of strength consists of 112 miles of biking, 2.4 miles of swimming through tough ocean waves, and a 26.2-mile marathon over challenging lava-covered terrain. This is a contest of endurance that will test the mettle of even the finest athletes in the world. The spiritual trial you're facing right now is much the same.

The Ironman competitors keep themselves in tip-top shape and train all year around for the one-day event. They consistently exercise, patiently building up their strength. They know strength training is a gradual process. A strong body isn't built overnight, and neither is a strong spirit. Jude 20 exhorts us to build ourselves up in our most holy faith, praying in the Holy Ghost.

Everyone has been given the measure of faith, just as every man and woman has been given muscles in their bodies. But that muscle will grow depending on how you build it up. You have to use that muscle if you expect to see it increase in strength. You might start with five-pound weights, then move up to ten pounds and later to twenty. You are building yourself up.

The same thing happens to your faith when you pray. You are building up your faith when you spend more and more time in prayer, taking your faith from glory to glory. I remember hearing giants of faith who have since moved to heaven, such as John Osteen and Lester Sumrall, say the problem with the body of Christ is that most believers will not pray ten minutes a day. But if they did, their lives would radically change.

Once you have prayed, keep yourself rooted in the love of God. Stay focused on His promises. This is not the time to be indecisive. James 1:6 says, "But let him ask in faith, nothing wavering. For he that wavereth is like a wave of the sea driven with the wind and tossed" (KJV). But the kicker is the following verse: "For let not that man think that he shall receive any thing of the Lord" (v. 7, KJV). Wavering will cost you your winning position in prayer. The Lord cannot give you anything unless you make up your mind once and for all that He will answer your prayers. A person who doubts is like a wave that crests at one moment, only to crash at the next. One minute he believes, and another he does not. He says yes to what God says, then changes his mind and says no when he looks at the circumstances. He never makes up his mind about what he really believes. He staggers like a drunk, reeling from one side of the spectrum to the other. The man who doubts will not get his prayer answered, but the man who refuses to give up and continues to trust that God's Word is true will always receive from Him.

While you are waiting, look around for the other assignments God has for you. This is the best time to reach out to others in worse situations than yours. This is the time to take trophies along the way. The more people you help, the more children you pray for, the closer you are to getting your answer. So get busy and remember, your children are not "up for grabs" by dark forces! Stand strong against the enemy in the power of the blood of Jesus; Satan cannot have your children.

And when you are praising and worshiping God, take authority over unholy alliances your children may have formed with the world. These ungodly relationships were designed by the enemy to divert them from God's ways or the things He has for them. Matthew 16:19 says whatever we bind on earth will be bound in heaven, and everything we loose on earth will be loosed in heaven. We can command evil spirits to loose their control of our children.

Stand in the gap and place a hedge of protection around your children at all times. Revelation 12:11 says we overcome by the blood of Jesus and the word of our testimony. We have victory over the enemy because of the blood of Jesus. It has never lost its power.

Remind the enemy that a bloodline of protection has been drawn around your family, and he cannot cross it. God turns the hearts of kings whichever way He wills (Proverbs 21:1), and He is able to direct the heart of your child, no matter what they are involved in. He is a mighty God. He answers prayer in His timing, not ours, but His arm is not too short to save our offspring. His power knows no limit. Let's stand in faith and agree together for your children to return to the Lord.

> *Lord, I give myself totally over to You. My life, my body, my mind, and my children belong to You. I plead the blood of Jesus over my family and stand in the authority God has given me as a believer (Luke 10:19). I rebuke the work of the enemy in my children's lives. I declare that my children will serve You. I declare that any covenants my children have made with death shall be annulled. My children shall return from the enemy's land. Lord, thank You for placing a hedge of protection around my family. I praise You in advance for the victory. Thank You for Your strength and power and for Your great love for me and my family. I am going to praise and worship You and rejoice in Your goodness for as long as I live. In the mighty name of Jesus, amen.*

Dry, empty religion won't bring you the breakthrough you are seeking for. God wants to have a vibrant and living relationship with you, and that happens when you worship Him. Start praising the Lord and give yourself over to Him. Start telling Jesus how much you love Him. When you give Him all the worship and praise and rejoicing you can muster, the answer will come every time. God will do great and mighty things for you as you spend regular time in His presence—because that is where you will find your joy.

Appendix A

Scriptures to Pray Over Your Children

THE BIBLE SAYS we have all power over the enemy. Below are some excellent scriptures you can use to declare God's promises over your children and defeat the enemy's plans for your children.

Lord, I will teach my children to keep the ways of the Lord.

For I have known (chosen, acknowledged) him [as My own], so that he may teach and command his children and the sons of his house after him to keep the way of the Lord and to do what is just and righteous, so that the Lord may bring Abraham what He has promised him.

—GENESIS 18:19

Lord, I thank You that my children are blessed.

And He will love you and bless you and multiply you; He will
also bless the fruit of your womb.

—DEUTERONOMY 7:13, NKJV

Blessed shall be the fruit of your body.

—DEUTERONOMY 28:4, NKJV

Lord, may I walk in love toward my children, and let us love You with
all of our hearts.

The LORD *your God will change your heart and the hearts of*
all your descendants, so that you will love him with all your
heart and soul and so you may live!

—DEUTERONOMY 30:6, NLT

Lord, You have set life and death before us. I choose life and blessings.
My family will serve You. We will live and not die.

I call heaven and earth to witness this day against you that I
have set before you life and death, the blessings and the curses;
therefore choose life, that you and your descendants may live
and may love the Lord your God, obey His voice, and cling to
Him. For He is your life and the length of your days, that you

may dwell in the land which the Lord swore to give to your fathers, to Abraham, Isaac, and Jacob.

—DEUTERONOMY 30:19–20

Lord, I thank You that my children will not do iniquity but will walk in Your ways.

They also do no iniquity;

They walk in His ways.

—PSALM 119:3, NKJV

My child will heed Your Word and cleanse his way.

Wherewithal shall a young man cleanse his way? by taking heed thereto according to thy word.

—PSALM 119:9, KJV

Lord, my children are a blessing from You. They do not belong to the enemy.

Behold, children are a heritage from the Lord, the fruit of the womb a reward.

—PSALM 127:3

Lord, You will perfect that which concerns my family.

The LORD *will perfect that which concerneth me: thy mercy, O* LORD, *endureth for ever: forsake not the works of thine own hands.*

—PSALM 138:8, KJV

Lord, deliver my children from the way of evildoers.

Discretion shall preserve thee, understanding shall keep thee: To deliver thee from the way of the evil man, from the man that speaketh froward things; who leave the paths of uprightness, to walk in the ways of darkness; who rejoice to do evil, and delight in the frowardness of the wicked.

—PROVERBS 2:11–14, KJV

Lord, let Your Word light my children's path and keep them from evil.

My son, keep your father's [God-given] commandment and forsake not the law of [God] your mother [taught you]. . . When 172 *you go, they [the words of your parents' God] shall lead you;*

when you sleep, they shall keep you; and when you waken, they shall talk to you. For the commandment is a lamp, and the whole teaching [of the law] is light, and reproofs of discipline are a way of life, to keep you from the evil woman, from the flattery of the tongue of the loose woman.

—PROVERBS 6:20, 22–24

My children shall not depart from God.

Train up a child in the way he should go [and in keeping with his individual gift or bent], and when he is old he will not depart from it.

—PROVERBS 22:6

I annul any covenant my child has formed with death, and no agreement with hell shall stand.

And hail shall sweep away the refuge of lies, and the waters shall overflow the hiding place. And [insert your child's name] covenant with death shall be disannulled, and [their] agreement with hell shall not stand.

—ISAIAH 28:17–18, KJV

Lord, thank You for pouring out Your spirit on my children.

For I will pour water upon him that is thirsty, and floods upon the dry ground: I will pour my spirit upon thy seed, and my blessing upon thine offspring: And they shall spring up as among the grass, as willows by the water courses.

—ISAIAH 44:3-4, KJV

Thank You, Lord, for saving my children.

For I will contend with him who contends with you, and I will give safety to your children and ease them.

—ISAIAH 49:25

Great is the peace of my children.

And all your [spiritual] children shall be disciples [taught by the Lord and obedient to His will], and great shall be the peace and undisturbed composure of your children. You shall establish yourself in righteousness (rightness, in conformity with God's will and order): you shall be far from even the thought of oppression and destruction, for you shall not fear, and from terror, for it shall not come near you . . . But no weapon that is formed against you shall prosper, and every tongue that shall rise against you in judgment you shall show to be in the wrong.

*This [peace, righteousness, security, triumph over opposition] is
the heritage of the servants of the Lord.*

—Isaiah 54:13–14, 17

Lord, Your Word will not depart from my children's mouths.

As for me, this is my covenant with them, saith the Lord; *My
spirit that is upon thee, and my words which I have put in thy
mouth, shall not depart out of thy mouth, nor out of the mouth
of thy seed, nor out of the mouth of thy seed's seed, saith the*
Lord, *from henceforth and for ever.*

—Isaiah 59:21, kjv

My children are a blessing. They were not born for trouble.

They shall not labor in vain,
Nor bring forth children for trouble.
For they shall be the descendants of the blessed of the Lord,
And their offspring with them.

—Isaiah 65:23, nkjv

My children shall return from the land of the enemy.

Thus says the Lord: Restrain your voice from weeping and your eyes from tears, for your work shall be rewarded, says the Lord; and [your children] shall return from the enemy's land. And there is hope for your future, says the Lord; your children shall come back to their own country.

—JEREMIAH 31:16–17

My children belong to the Lord.

Believe in the Lord Jesus Christ [give yourself up to Him, take yourself out of your own keeping and entrust yourself into His keeping] and you will be saved, [and this applies both to] you and your household as well.

—ACTS 16:31

God, You are the author of simplicity, not confusion.

. . . the simplicity that is in Christ.

—2 CORINTHIANS 11:3, KJV

Lord, keep my children from the unfruitful works of darkness.

And have no fellowship with the unfruitful works of darkness, but rather reprove them. For it is a shame even to speak of those things which are done of them in secret.

—Ephesians 5:11–12, kjv

Lord, I will not provoke my children to anger but will rear them in the counsel of the Lord.

Fathers, do not irritate and provoke your children to anger [do not exasperate them to resentment], but rear them [tenderly] in the training and discipline and the counsel and admonition of the Lord.

—Ephesians 6:4

Lord, guard my children from fleshly lusts.

Beloved, I beg you as sojourners and pilgrims, abstain from fleshly lusts which war against the soul, having your conduct honorable among the Gentiles, that when they speak against you as evildoers, they may, by your good works which they observe, glorify God in the day of visitation.

—1 Peter 2:11–12, nkjv

Joyful Parent

APPENDIX B

Prayer of Salvation

YOU WON'T EXPERIENCE all God wants for your family if you don't know Him personally. Many people think they wil go to heven jut because they attend church. It amazes us after 35 years of ministry that this attitude still prevails. But that is why you have to continue to teach the Word over and over again, since there are always new ears to hear. The Bible says, "If you acknowledge and confess with your lips that Jesus is Lord and in your heart believe (adhere to, trust in, and rely on the truth) that God raised Him from the dead, you will be saved. For with the heart a person believes (adheres to, trusts in, and relies on Christ) and so is justified (declared righteous, acceptable to God), and with the mouth he confesses (declares openly and speaks out freely his faith) and confirms [his] salvation" (Romans 10:9–10).

If you have never accepted Jesus as your personal Lord and Savior, today is your day. All you have to do is pray this prayer:

Dear Lord Jesus,

I know that I am a sinner, and I am lost without You. I believe You died on the cross for my sins and rose from the grave on the third day. I also know that

You paid for the penalty for all my sins through Your sacrifice. I accept Your free gift of eternal life. Thank You for saving me.

Amen.

Notes

Chapter 1
Joy Is Your Strength

Merriam-Webster's Collegiate Dictionary, 11th edition (Springfield, MA: Merriam-Webster, 2003), s.v. "depression."

Chapter 2
Relentless Love

Kenneth E. Hagin, *Love: The Way to Victory* (Tulsa, OK: Faith Library Publications, 1994), 85–89. Used with permission. www.rhema.org.

Chapter 3
These Are Not Your Daughter's Jeans

Harry Bradford, "10 Fastest Growing U.S. Industries: IBISWorld," *Huffington Post*, July 18, 2011, http://www
.huffingtonpost.com/2011/05/18/ten-growing-industries
-ibisworld_n_862754.html#s279469&title=6_Correctional
_Facilities (accessed January 12, 2012).

Chapter 4
Believe God for the Victory

Merriam-Webster's Collegiate Dictionary, s.v. "courage."

Francis McGaw, *Praying Hyde* (Grand Rapids, MI: Bethany House Publishers, 1970).

Chapter 5
A Choice to Rejoice

Lillian Kwon, "Outreach Releases Largest, Fastest-Growing Churches Report," ChristianPost.com, September 13, 2011, http://www.christianpost.com/news/outreach-releases-largest-fastest-growing-churches-report-55572/ (accessed January 12, 2012).

CHAPTER 6
GET REFOCUSED

David Yonggi Cho and R. Whitney Manzano, *The Fourth Dimension* (Alachua, FL: Bridge-Logos Publishers, 1979).

2. TheFix.com, "The 10 Most Wasted Nations on Earth: France, Prescription Pills," *TheFix.com*, June 11, 2011, http://www.thefix.com/content/top-10-addicted-countries-0#slide2 (accessed January 13, 2012).

"Depression Rates Higher in Wealthy Countries, Study Finds," *The Independent*, July 26, 2011, http://www.independent.co.uk/life-style/health-and-families/depression-rates-higher-in-wealthy-countries-study-finds-2326414.html (accessed January 13, 2012).

CHAPTER 8
SHOUT IT OUT

Merriam-Webster's Collegiate Dictionary, s.v., "rest."

Ibid.

Troy Anderson, "L.A. Dream Center Will Help Many Hurt by Recession," *Daily News*, September 6, 2010, http://www.dailynews.com/ci_16006279 (accessed January 13, 2012).

DreamCenter.org, "About Us," http://www.dreamcenter.org/about-us/ (accessed January 13, 2012).

CHAPTER 11
SHAKE IT OFF

WebMD.com, "Snakebite: Symptoms of a Pit Viper Bite," June 18, 2010, http://www.webmd.com/a-to-z-guides/snakebite-symptoms-of-a-pit-viper-bite-topic-overview (accessed January 16, 2012).

Barry S. Gold, Richard C. Dart, and Robert A. Barish, "Bites of Venomous Snakes," *New England Journal of Medicine* 347 (April 1, 2002): 347–356, http://www.nejm.org/doi/full/10.1056/NEJMra013477?siteid=nejm&keytype=ref&ijkey=%2FRomzox5%2FYq3A (preview accessed January 16, 2012).

Smith Wigglesworth, "Faith Laughs at Impossibilities," Daily Devotional—Smith Wigglesworth Devotional, January 16, 2010, *Charismamag.com*, http://www.charismamag.com/index.php/daily-devotionals/1062-smith-wigglesworth-devotional-/25973-faith-laughs-at-impossibilities (accessed January 17, 2012).

Chapter 14
Rest and Rejoice

Shannon Byrne, in discussion with the author, December 2011. Used with permission.

Alice Gossett, in discussion with the author, December 2011. Used with permission.

The Harrison House Vision

Proclaiming the truth and the power

Of the Gospel of Jesus Christ

With excellence;

Challenging Christians to

Live victoriously,

Grow spiritually,

Know God intimately.